THE GOTHAM LIBRARY
OF THE NEW YORK UNIVERSITY PRESS

The Gotham Library is a series of original works and critical studies, published in paperback primarily for student use. The Gotham hardcover edition is primarily for use by libraries and the general reader. Devoted to significant works and major authors and to literary topics of enduring importance, Gotham Library texts offer the best in literature and criticism.

Comparative and Foreign Language Literature:
Robert J. Clements, Editor
Comparative and English Language Literature:
James W. Tuttleton, Editor

Candles and Carnival Lights:

The Catholic Sensibility of F. Scott Fitzgerald

Joan M. Allen

New York · New York University Press · 1978

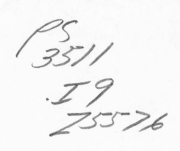

Copyright © 1978 by New York University

Library of Congress Cataloging in Publication Data

Allen, Joan M.   1938-
   Candles and carnival lights.

   (The Gotham library of the New York University Press)
   Includes bibliographical references and index.
   1. Fitzgerald, Francis Scott Key, 1896-1940.
   2, Fitzgerald, Francis Scott Key, 1896-1940—Religion
   and ethics. 3. Novelists, American—20th century—
   Biography. I. Title.
   PS3511.I9Z5576   813'.5'2 [B]   77-82752
   ISBN 0-8147-0563-4
   ISBN 0-8147-0564-2 pbk.

Manufactured in the United States of America

for Dot

Permissions

All quotations from the works of F. Scott Fitzgerald are used with the permission of Charles Scribner's Sons, and are fully protected by copyright. Permission has been granted to quote from several other books: F. Scott Fitzgerald, *The Crack-Up*, Copyright 1936 by Esquire, Inc., copyright 1945 by New Directions Publishing Corporation. Reprinted by permission of New Directions Publishing Corporation; Tony Buttitta, *After the Good Gay Times*, copyright © 1974 by Anthony Buttitta, all rights reserved, first published by The Viking Press, Inc.; Kenneth E. Eble, *F. Scott Fitzgerald*, Twayne Publishers; Sheilah Graham, *The Real F. Scott Fitzgerald Thirty-Five Years Later*, copyright © 1976 by Sheilah Graham, all rights reserved, Grossett & Dunlap, Inc., publisher; Shane Leslie, *Long Shadows*, John Murray (Publishers) Ltd.; Sara Mayfield, *Exiles from Paradise*, Delacorte Press, Inc.; Nancy Milford, *Zelda: A Biography*, Harper & Row Publishers, Inc.; Arthur Mizener, *The Far Side of Paradise*, Houghton Mifflin Company; Milton Stern, *The Golden Moment: The Novels of F. Scott Fitzgerald*, University of Illinois Press. I am deeply grateful to Mrs. C. Grove Smith for permission to quote from *The Apprentice Fiction of F. Scott Fitzgerald*, ed. John Kuehl, Rutgers University Press, and to Matthew J. Bruccoli for permission to quote from *F. Scott Fitzgerald's Ledger*, A Bruccoli Clark Book, and from Elizabeth Beckwith Mackie's "My Friend Scott Fitzgerald," *Fitzgerald/Hemingway Annual 1970*.

Portions of this book, in altered form, have appeared in the *Fitzgerald/Hemingway Annual* (1973, 1974).

Contents

Preface   xi

Acknowledgments   xv

1. A USABLE PAST

The Early Years: 1909-1911—Buffalo and St. Paul   1
Literary Apprenticeship: 1911-1917—The Newman
School and Princeton   25

2 EARLY SUCCESS: 1917-1920   54

This Side of Paradise   62

3 THE SAD YOUNG MAN: 1920-1924   84

"Absolution"   93
The Great Gatsby   101

4 THE LOST DECADE: 1924-1934   117

Tender Is the Night   124

5   THE LAST YEARS: 1935-1940   132

    Confessional Pieces and Letters   133
    Hollywood: *The Last Tycoon*   137

    Notes   146

    The Fitzgerald Papers   157

    Index   159

Preface

The statement this book makes about F. Scott Fitzgerald has evolved from the time when, as an undergraduate, I read *This Side of Paradise*. My own romantic notions about Princeton and the academic life made this novel special for me. Later I came to prefer the consummate artistry of *The Great Gatsby* and the chaotic and mature pain of *Tender Is the Night* to the sophomoric self-indulgence of the first novel, but I still admired its exuberance. I could not shake my first intuitive response to something elusive yet very Catholic and thus familiar to me in it and in the other novels and stories, as I read in the biographies and criticism about the man who had delineated the American experience, the temper of the Jazz Age, and the lostness of his generation. He had done that, but there was something else that tenaciously held my puzzled interest. Some critics claimed for him a sort of romantic moralism, and this came closer to the mark.

All of my intriguing questions about Fitzgerald—his prominent theme of parents' failures to nurture the spirits of their children, his heroes who either adopt surrogate fathers who are priests or assume the priestly role themselves, his viciously destructive women who wear masks designed to hide their essential insidiousness, his men who allow themselves to be emasculated by these fascinating destroyers, the abundant squeamishness about sex in a writer proclaimed as risqué and shocking, the ubiquitous carnival imagery in his writing—I speculated might be answered in the light of his Roman Catholic experience. The image of Gatsby standing on his lawn in his pose of yearning and benediction had been at the center of all of my thinking about Fitzgerald's work; I suspected that this image and Gatsby's strangely sexless passion were somehow related. When I read "Absolution" and learned that Fitzgerald had once considered it the story of the young Gatsby, but had deleted it from the book to preserve a sense of mystery about his hero, my suspicion was confirmed, and the investigation leading to this book began. "Absolution" seemed to me to be a germinal work in understanding the profusion of Catholic language and imagery and habits of response in Fitzgerald's writing.

I do not discount the importance of Fitzgerald as a social historian, nor do I suggest that his Roman Catholicism is the key to his writing. I accept the validity of several other approaches to his work, and in this book I do not attempt to preclude them. Rather I have looked very closely at the evidence of Catholic influence in Fitzgerald's life and work, and here I lay out that evidence for consideration. My purpose is to show that his Roman Catholic early education and family experiences, the complexities of a Catholic upbringing in an atmosphere of inadequate paternity and oppressive maternity and ambivalence about money, formed his moral consciousness. Fitzgerald's Catholicism, I believe, was as influential as the whole complex of his troubled family background—indeed, it cannot be separated from that background—in determining his literary themes, characterizations, and style. But a man's life is not so easily dissected. An artist's life, and Fitzgerald's is no exception, is rich in incident, motivation, and influence. To point with certainty to one component and to claim that this is the key, the rationale for the total man, is folly. Fitzgerald himself said: "There never was a good biography of a good novelist. There couldn't be. He is too many people, if he's any good." [1] I concur, and I offer this book, not as a substitute for other books about Fitzgerald, but as a companion piece which opens up a dimension of the man and writer that has too long been ignored.

One reason why most critics have ignored Fitzgerald's Irish Catholicism is the fact that he successfully hid it from a predominantly WASP public which found it not socially acceptable. He was the first Irish Catholic to become a major American novelist, and he was a member of the first generation of American writers who earned their living from their writing. He had a genius for public relations and image-making and also a consciousness of himself and his writing as salable commodities. Today, Fitzgerald, a closet Catholic, could proudly come out to join writers like Wilfred Sheed, Walker Percy, Graham Greene, Brian Moore, Elizabeth Cullinan, Thomas Keneally, Garry Wills, and Tom McHale, who have communicated the Catholic experience to a reading public suddenly interested in hearing about the arcane life-style of a group they had in turn feared, hated, and ridiculed. I think he would have enjoyed the idea of the post-Vatican Council II Roman Catholic church as a romantic lost cause and that he would have joined the faction nostalgic for the Latin Mass and the security of the old religion against those morbidly fascinated by the widening crack in the Vatican.

The title of this book means to suggest Fitzgerald's divided nature. The appearances of his life and work, the lights of the carnival which attracted and destroyed him and his fictional brothers, the apparently glamorous life, is one component. But that masks his profound moralism, the realization of sin and destructiveness which underlie and permeate the temporal world. The carnival lights outshone the candles, but the candles had indelibly touched him, and some of the language, characterizations, and moral concerns in his work are evidence of this.

There was no happy reconciliation of these two warring strains in Fitzgerald. He and his characters were crippled by an immoderate materialism and melancholy, and their yearning for a realization of some idealistic, spiritual existence was never consummated. This is the tension in Fitzgerald's work which saves him from being frivolous and dated. Fitzgerald was not a practicing Catholic for all of his life, nor was he a Catholic novelist in a literal sense. But the man whose major theme was the vanity of worldly dreams was possessed of a profoundly religious, if confused, sensibility, and that sensibility derived largely from his Catholic experience. It is this experience and its effects which this book examines.

Acknowledgments

The gathering of evidence for and the writing of this book would have been impossible without the help of countless people. A few must have special mention and thanks.

I am indebted to Matthew J. Bruccoli, Sara Mayfield, Arthur Mizener, and Henry Dan Piper for their generous responses to my queries; Mrs. C. Grove Smith ("Scottie"), Mrs. Clifton Sprague (Annabel Fitzgerald), Judge John Biggs, Jr., and Charles Marquis Warren for their personal reminiscences of Fitzgerald; Father Clyde Eddy, St. Paul Seminary, who supplied me with materials and several leads in my literary detective work; Miss Irene Barron, who kindly shared with me the stories of her family, some of the history of the Catholic church in St. Paul, and her brother's relationship with the McQuillans and the Fitzgeralds; spokesmen for the Archdioceses of Baltimore, New York, St. Paul and Minneapolis, Seattle, and Washington, D.C.; spokesmen for the Dioceses of Buffalo and Syracuse; Margaret Benner, D.H.M., Nardin Academy; Sister Margaret Mary Burke, Convent of the Visitation; the Reverend William P. Heffernan, M.M.; Sister Kathleen, Holy Angels School; Hugh A. Kennedy, S.J.; Vicar-General Andrew P. Mahoney, Oblates of Mary Immaculate, for much hard information; Alexander P. Clark, Curator of Manuscripts, and Mrs. Wanda Randall, who extended me every

xv

courtesy and generous assistance in my work at the Princeton University Library; John Hicks and Robert Tucker, who have seen me through this project with endless words of good cheer and sound guidance; Dorothea B. Lillie, and Constance K. Weaver for their encouragement and help. The picture of Fitzgerald is used with the permission of Mrs. C. Grove Smith and Princeton University.

1.

A Usable Past

The Early Years: 1909–1911
Buffalo and St. Paul

Scott Fitzgerald was an Irish Catholic. What were some of the effects of this ineradicable fact of biography in Fitzgerald's thought and life, and how did it influence his work as an artist? That Fitzgerald was an Irish Catholic raised in a provincial milieu largely by devoutly religious convent-educated women both in his schools and at home, that the Catholic father of this household was a universally acknowledged failure whom Fitzgerald in his maturity nevertheless deeply loved, that the father also greatly influenced the romanticism of his son—all this, as we shall see, profoundly affected Fitzgerald the writer. Fitzgerald's Catholicism is not the whole story, to be sure. The repressive and puritanical cultural mores which prevailed in this country at the turn of the century and which both affected and were affected by the moral posture of the Roman Catholic Church, the subject of another discussion, were certainly influential forces in Fitzgerald's background. But his Catholic family and upbringing in a Catholic city, and especially a parochial school education, etched attitudes and patterns of response in Fitzgerald's psyche that remained with him throughout his life, altered or modified sometimes, or sometimes suppressed, but never wholly expunged.

1

Fitzgerald's story began in the city of St. Paul, whose promise of fortune drew his parents to it by separate ways. His mother, Mollie, was the eldest child of Philip Francis McQuillan, an Irish immigrant who had settled in St. Paul in 1857 when it still had the look and aroma of a frontier trading post. P. F., as he was called, worked for a time as a clerk before he began his own business, which ultimately grew into one of the largest wholesale grocery concerns in the city. When P. F. died in 1877 at the age of forty-three, he had amassed a personal fortune of over a quarter of a million dollars and had established a multi-million-dollar business. Through their generosity, the McQuillans became one of the leading Catholic families in St. Paul. P. F. contributed generously to the construction of St. Mary's Church in 1866, and he served on the board of the St. Mary's Home for Friendless Girls.[1] On the day of P. F.'s funeral, the children of the Catholic Orphans Home, which counted him as one of its major benefactors, were among the multitude of mourners. P. F. had also been instrumental in bringing the Sisters of the Visitation of St. Louis to St. Paul a few years before his death.[2] Their convent and academy, which in various ways served three generations of McQuillans and Fitzgeralds, were built for them by the daughter of James J. Hill. Fitzgerald's mother and sister attended the Convent of the Visitation; his nieces spent some time there during World War II;[3] and his daughter was baptized at the convent at the request of her Grandmother Fitzgerald, who was a great friend and benefactor of the nuns all her life. Because P. F. had been in wholesale business rather than in retail trade, his family found a relatively respectable position in St. Paul society.[4] But the McQuillans had no great social ambition; they were content to be considered a financially sound and pious Catholic family. Mollie McQuillan received a convent education and acquired some measure of sophistication in four family excursions to Europe planned by her mother primarily to pay their respects to the Pope. Mollie was a voracious though not a discriminating reader, a characteristic noted by her son in a sketch written after her death, "An Author's Mother." She was more interested in men than her spinster sisters were, and she was eager to marry, but she was not especially physically attractive. At thirty, after some disappointments, with no other prospects in view, she married Edward Fitzgerald, a man she had known for several years.

Edward Fitzgerald was born in 1853 near Rockville, Maryland, into an aristocratic though apparently not affluent family. His father is an obscure figure, but his mother was a descendant of fine old families of the colony and of England. Fitzgerald was named for her most notable ancestor, Francis Scott Key, the brother of her great-grandfather. The area in which Edward Fitzgerald grew up was sympathetic to the South in the Civil War, an event which would remain the great romance of his life. As a boy Scott asked him repeatedly to tell how he had helped to transport Confederate spies and about the march of southern troops toward Washington in the last days of the war. After three years of high school at Georgetown, Edward Fitzgerald went west, stopping in Chicago for a time before he went on to St. Paul to head a small wicker-furniture business. He was a small, reserved, courtly, meticulously turned out man, and his southern manners and gentle pace were not suited to the bustling atmosphere of the Midwest. To his son it seemed that he came from "tired, old stock," and that he had been destined for failure. Certainly the vitality of the marriage of Mollie McQuillan and "Ted" Fitzgerald was the wife's sole province. They were married in 1890, as gossip had it, after she had forced him to it by threatening to jump into the Mississippi if he did not propose. They went abroad for their wedding trip and then returned to St. Paul to begin their family. Within six years they had two daughters, who were to die three months before their only son was born. Their misfortune was compounded a year and a half later when the wicker-furniture business failed, and the family moved to Buffalo, where Fitzgerald worked as a salesman for Procter and Gamble.

This is the situation into which Scott Fitzgerald was born. McQuillan-Fitzgerald antitheses, which affected his attitudes and ultimately his work, had already been struck in his life: vitality and fatigued gentility, aggressive self-made success and failure, the pragmatic and the romantic, the assurance of the established and the tentativeness of the outsider. But one of the few things the

McQuillans and the Fitzgeralds held in common, their Roman Catholicism, profoundly influenced Fitzgerald in his boyhood and ever after.

Scott Fitzgerald was born in St. Paul on September 24, 1896, and he was baptized either eleven or twelve days later. His mother noted the date as October 5 in the baby book she kept for him,[5] while the Cathedral of St. Paul record shows that he was baptized on October 6 by the Reverend J. T. Harrison, pastor of St. Joseph's Church, a parish which shortly thereafter merged with the neighboring cathedral. His godparents were Phillip McQuillan, his mother's brother, and Emily Harden. The Fitzgeralds stayed in St. Paul until 1898 when they moved to Buffalo for the first time. After three years there, Edward Fitzgerald was transferred by Procter and Gamble to Syracuse, where Fitzgerald's sister, Annabel, was born. In 1903, Edward Fitzgerald's job once more took the family to Buffalo, and here they remained for five years. In Buffalo, Fitzgerald probably entered into the second phase of his formal association with the church, for in 1903 he had reached the "age of reason," seven years, when a young Catholic customarily receives the sacrament of Holy Communion for the first time. Because of the Fitzgeralds' irregular arrangement with the Holy Angels Convent, no records concerning Scott were kept.[6] (Apparently he had been disturbed by an earlier attempt in Syracuse to place him in school. His parents thought it best to humor him and allow him daily to choose the session which he preferred to attend.) But surely the future altar boy and son of a pious Catholic mother conformed to the usual pattern of sacramental observance.

In his preparations for receiving the sacraments, Fitzgerald began to feel the influence of St. Augustine, whose writings form the basis of much of Western theology and specifically the dogma of the Roman Catholic Church. Fitzgerald certainly read some of Augustine's work in his philosophy and theology courses at the Newman School, and we know that Augustine was one of the models Monsignor Fay held up to Fitzgerald in his attempts to demonstrate that the Church had produced great and even glamorous men. But even if Fitzgerald had never heard Augustine's name, still he was inevitably influenced by the teachings of Augustine, for they have been retained in large measure in the catechisms used in educating young Catholics.

Augustine of Hippo (354-430), before his conversion to Christianity from Manichaeanism, to which sect he belonged for nine years, was a teacher of rhetoric in Carthage, Rome, and Milan. As a young man he led a dissolute life, which displeased his devoutly Christian mother, Monica, who herself is a saint of the Church. The ambitious and decidedly secular Augustine was living in Milan with his mistress and their son when the direction of his life was changed. In Carthage, Augustine had associated Christianity with the poor, but here he met wealthy Christians like Ambrose, who had renounced his position to become the bishop of Milan. Monsignor Fay undoubtedly did not fail to point to the parallels in Augustine's and Fitzgerald's backgrounds—the strong mother, the tendency to luxury, the mistaken notion as to the possibilities for success within the Church. Augustine returned to Carthage hoping to lead a monastic life, but this was not possible, for he was much in demand as a preacher and consultant on church affairs, and finally he entered the hierarchy of the Church when he became bishop of Hippo in 397.

Augustine's best-known writings are his *Confessions,* a remarkable work in which he recounts his early life and his conversion to Christianity, considered by many the first autobiography in the modern sense, and *The City of God.* The latter, which contains a summary of Christian doctrine and a view of history to which the Church still holds—namely, that the entire world from beginning to end has, as its end, the constitution of a holy society—was Augustine's answer to those who blamed the fall of Rome on Christianity. The decadence of the Holy Roman Empire antedated Christianity, Augustine asserted, and it was insufficient rather than too much Christian influence which had hastened its decay. Augustine's purpose in *The City of God* was more than merely to vindicate the Church. He recognized that something new was needed to shore it up against attacks which would increase and become more effective as the Church grew and became unwieldy. The days of the undogmatic Church when simple belief in the Gospels was enough to sustain the relatively small Christian community had passed. Using the intellectual tools developed by

Greek philosophers, his own training as a Manichaean, and the Roman legalistic habit of mind he had absorbed as a rhetorician, he formulated a creed and influenced the institution of a strong ecclesiastical organization the Church would need in order to survive in the post-Roman world. The process of the creation of dogma extended through several ages, and the work of Augustine marked a transition between the contructive period of Christian thought and the Middle Ages when dogma became fixed. Orthodoxy, an infallible system based upon legalistic authority, is what Augustine gave to subsequent ages of Christianity in *The City of God.*

As well as his dualistic metaphor of two diverse cities, some of the dogma Augustine set down in this seminal work of Christianity are current even today and have helped to form many of the attitudes of Catholics like Fitzgerald. Augustine wrote that salvation was possible only within the Church, a dogma which has fostered a sense of exclusivity in Catholics with which Fitzgerald suffered, and which was manifested in his own posture as an outsider and in many of his characters. Augustine also articulated the dogmata of Original Sin and Grace which are learned by every Catholic child. Before the fall, according to Augustine, Adam was free, but his apostasy corrupted human nature and the race subsequently lost its power of free action. Man is therefore predetermined to sin, which he cannot escape but by the supernatural aid of God's grace, which comes only through the Church in the rite of baptism. Augustine's and subsequently the Church's and Fitzgerald's attitude toward sex is an important component of the dogma of Original Sin and consequently of the Catholic experience. In Adam's fall we sinned all, as the Puritans said, who adopted this Augustinian tenet along with the doctrine of predestination. Women pull down from their spirituality men who strive for purity. Sex is legitimate only for purposes of procreation, and even within marriage sex is essentially shameful, for it is a thing of privacy and darkness. These attitudes account for the Church's teaching about the superiority of celibacy and the inferiority of women since they are ever the occasions of sin.

This tendency to regard the body as naturally evil and apart from God and the consequent impulse to the ascetic life early gained a foothold in the Church and antedated Augustine. But in his elaboration of the City of Man-City of God metaphor he did much to establish the antagonism between the life of the flesh and the life of the spirit in Western Christianity. This antithesis is at the root of his metaphor of the two cities, and it was probably influenced by Augustine's earlier adherence to Manichaeanism, the principal doctrine of which concerned the conflict between Light (goodness) and Darkness (chaos or evil). Set in opposition in Augustine's earthly and heavenly cities are love of the world and the flesh and love of God and the spirit, tempestuousness and serenity, the wicked and the just, disorder and order, rivalry with God and submission to God, Babylon and Jerusalem. This is the sort of antithesis we see as well in the works of Fitzgerald.

We do have concrete evidence of Fitzgerald's church attendance in a 1903 entry in his Ledger:[7] "He fell under the spell of a Catholic preacher, Father Fallon, of the Church of the Holy Angels" (158). Occasionally Fitzgerald was impressed by dynamic priests, and in this case the boy of seven apparently had discerning taste, for the Reverend Michael Fallon was no ordinary parish priest. He was a native Canadian who studied at Ottawa University, which is run by the Oblates of Mary Immaculate, the order in which he would serve as the first provincial of the Eastern American Province in Buffalo. Apparently marked for leadership by his order, Fallon was sent to Rome for postgraduate study, and there he earned the degree of Doctor of Sacred Theology and was ordained by the cardinal-vicar of Rome in 1894. Upon his return to Ottawa, Fallon taught English at the University. The sermons that later would mesmerize the young Fitzgerald were produced by a man skilled in the uses of rhetoric, one who could support a moral point with patristic allusions and passages from the great English poets. This is not typical Catholic fare, and Fitzgerald's reaction to it was not typically childish. As later he would be attracted to and instructed by the erudition of Edmund Wilson and John Peale Bishop, so at seven perhaps he intuitively knew that Fallon was a rare Catholic preacher, one who delivered a message of learning and substance with dramatic flair.

Fallon's career was distinguished in every way. A Catholic

pastor's measurable success is determined largely by the number and size of the buildings he erects. In 1901 the young priest went to Holy Angels Church in Buffalo in the dual role of pastor and provincial, and in his nine years there he was responsible for the building of the Oblate House near Catholic University in Washington, D.C., and the Holy Angels School in Buffalo. Fallon was elevated to the hierarchy when in 1910 at the age of forty-three he was appointed bishop of London, Ontario. His career there was marked by two notable accomplishments: the establishment of St. Peter's Seminary in London, one of the few English seminaries in Canada; and the establishment of training schools for bilingual teachers. Fallon opposed bilingual schools in his diocese because they did not adequately prepare teachers to teach either English or French. The matter of language was and still is a hotly partisan issue in Ontario, and Fallon's criticism of the schools brought him under the fire of the French-Canadians. He persisted in his view, however, and persuaded the government of Ontario to provide the training schools which effected great improvement in language instruction.

Fallon was known as an educator, an excellent English scholar, and a distinguished preacher and public speaker both in Canada and in the United States. It is clear why this tall, handsome, magnetic man with a voice perfectly suited to oratory was the object of Fitzgerald's admiration.

Another entry in Fitzgerald's Ledger tells us that in 1905 he "passed from the Holy Angels Academy to Miss Nardins" (160). Miss Nardins Academy was founded by a member of the Society of the Daughters of the Heart of Mary, a religious order that had been instituted in France in 1790. Miss Ernestine Nardin, the first superior of the Buffalo convent and academy, because of her distinguished academic career in Paris, had been asked to join the first emigration of society members to the United States. They established the first Catholic orphanage in Cleveland before Bishop Timon of Buffalo invited the order to his city. The women operated several parochial schools and free schools for the poor, but Miss Nardins Academy was the choice of the prosperous Catholic families of Buffalo. The academy, which was opened in 1858, followed a traditional American Catholic curriculum which included Greek, Latin, French, zoology, music, and art.[9] The continental manner of Miss Nardin, her order (which allowed its members to retain their family names), and her school must have strongly appealed to Mollie Fitzgerald. She bitterly resented the fall from status her husband's business failures had caused, and she was determined that her son would suffer no social disadvantage because of them.

Fitzgerald recorded in his Ledger that it was during his time at Miss Nardins that he wrote "a celebrated essay" on George Washington and St. Ignatius, an appropriate pair, since the sixteenth-century priest and scholar who founded the Society of Jesus was also a distinguished soldier. Fitzgerald also recorded the fact that he had lied in confession and that "in church one little girl made him frightfully embarrassed when he didn't have a penny to put in the collection box" (162). Fitzgerald was to use this incident first in "Absolution" and later in *Tender Is the Night,* where its hitherto inchoate significance is fully realized when Dick Diver recalls it in the context of what his relationship with Nicole and her money has been. A boy embarrassed by a female because of his lack of money is a recurrent configuration in much of Fitzgerald's work. The fact that the incident occurred in a church and was first used in an overtly Catholic story does not mean that it has religious significance. It does suggest, however, that a Catholic background cannot be separated from the emotional life of Fitzgerald's major male characters and that, even though it fades, it remains indelible.

Fitzgerald's writing career began in Buffalo with an incomplete history of the United States, which went only so far as the Battle of Bunker Hill, and an imitation of *Ivanhoe* called "Elavoe." But one must look ahead in Fitzgerald's writing for the fictional account of his adolescence to the Basil stories, which were written in 1928-29, for his literary apprenticeship goes back to the years in Buffalo, St. Paul, and at the Newman School. For all of the puritanical indoctrination to which Fitzgerald apparently was subjected, he was a sexually precocious child. His ability to discern the motivations of other children and his vocabulary were impressive to the older boys and girls whose relationships with one another aroused his curiosity. He began to understand their sexual activities with the onset of his early adolescence and his own romance with a dancing-school partner who was also his consort in kissing games; he used this Buffalo experience in one of the Basil stories, "That Kind of Party." [10] It gives us the picture of Fitzgerald at age ten, estranged from his parents, secretive and reluctant to expose his emotional life to them, and burdened with an acute sense of sin. Fitzgerald changed the names of the characters in this Basil story because it had been rejected by the editors of the *Saturday Evening Post*—who had published the others—because they believed that young children did not play the games Fitzgerald described. He hoped that disassociating "That Kind of Party" from the others would make it salable elsewhere.

The towheaded, green-eyed Terence R. Tipton, with his Irish name and Catholic conscience, is an obvious counterpart of Fitzgerald. He imagines himself a renowned actor, athlete, scholar, philatelist, and collector of cigar bands, but as the story begins he has left these boyish things behind. He has attended a party at which the major diversion has been kissing games; he has experienced for the first time one of life's "major compulsions," and he had become an addict in an hour. His desire to repeat the experience with the ten-year-old masked siren, Dolly Bartlett, a "precocious mistress" of seductive artifices, becomes obsessive. Dolly Bartlett is one of Fitzgerald's female destroyers, the *femmes fatales* or vampires, who wear masks of various sorts which are sure signals of their insidiousness. Fitzgerald was perhaps influenced by the Augustinian view of sexuality and women in his creation of his female characters. In Fitzgerald's writing the mask is either one of a group of expressions that can be called up at will, or it is constructed of powder and paint. It is either a tool of deception used consciously or a device of such long standing in the woman's arsenal that it has become a "natural" part of her equipment. The man against whom it is used is attracted to, and usually recognizes the mask for what it is; moreover, he admires the woman's prowess in its use. Fitzgerald's male grants the female destroyer the right to ruin him in this curious campaign in which the conventional sexual roles are reversed and he is the willing prey. This is the basic pattern of all the sexual relationships in Fitzgerald's published work, and the mask is usually the signpost which announces it. The device of the mask seems to have first occurred to Fitzgerald when he was nineteen and turned his attention to the social education of his younger sister, Annabel,[11] and thus began his lifelong practice of using the experiences of the women in his life as material for his writing. He wrote detailed instructions for her about conversation with boys; how to walk, dance, dress; and how to create a controlled facial expression. He told her, "It ought to be almost like a *mask*. . . . You'll have to use it in society and when you've practiced a thing in calm, then only are you sure of it as a good *weapon*" (emphasis mine).[12] Thereafter Fitzgerald's descriptions of his *femmes fatales* included some mention of their contrived artificiality, and almost always he used the image of the mask.[13]

Just as Fitzgerald's mature heroes are captivated by masked sirens, so Terence is bewitched by the allure of Dolly Bartlett. He rejects his mother's suggestion that she have a party for him because he does not want her to witness his lust; instead he persuades a friend to have the party at his house, but the girls will not cooperate in creating the "orgy" which Terence vividly paints in his imagination. The party is climaxed by a quasi-religious experience when a priggish, self-righteous boy who had been paralyzed for years falls from his wheelchair during an altercation with Terence. When the cripple walks, Terence becomes a Christ figure who must be viewed ironically. This "miracle" is God's way of reminding Terence of how depraved he really is, for he had sinned grievously in thought, word, and deed. Aside from his lust, which he had vaguely hoped to consummate with Dolly, earlier in the day he had punched and broken the glasses of a boy who had teased him, and he had sent a fake telegram in order to get his friend's mother out of the house during the party. Terence is heavy with the sense of sin, guilt, and retribution.

> He knew . . . he had sinned, and for a time he had walked . . . an alley [his Via Dolorosa] saying "Now I lay mes" over and over for worldly mercy in the matter of Albert Moore's spectacles. The rest could wait until he was found out, preferably after death. (173)

After a few hasty Our Fathers in the alley, Terence prepares to face retribution at home, but his telegram had been diverted to his own mother. He is saved for the moment, and a dinner invitation from

Dolly Bartlett further postpones his inevitable punishment. He thinks that it is time things went better after a day in which he had been insolent, committed forgery, and assaulted both the crippled and the blind. Even though he knows that his punishment will come in this life, for a time he will forget his guilt as he luxuriates in Dolly's company. Just as Rudolph Miller in "Absolution" knows that there is something gorgeous somewhere that has nothing to do with God, the deceptively alluring City of Man, so Terence seized the "one Blessed hour" that may compensate for his loss of grace and worldly mercy. But even though Terence and Fitzgerald's other heroes ultimately reject religion as a tenable force in their lives, they are not able to escape the habit of guilt.

Just as Terence is estranged from his family, Fitzgerald's relationship with his parents was always an uneasy one. In his first bit of correspondence on record, written to his mother in 1907 while he was at a summer camp, he said:

> I received your letter this morning and thought I would like very much to have you up here. I don't think you would like it as you know no one here. There are some very nice boarding houses but about the only fare is lamb and beef. I don't think you would like the accommodations as it is only a small town and no good hotels. Please send me a dollar because there are a lot of little odds and ends I need. I will spend it cautiously. All the other boys have pocket money besides their regular allowance.[14]

Even though he cleverly attempted to soften the essence of his message, it is clear that he simply did not want his mother to visit him, for he knew already that she was a social liability for him. Her insistence that the family move a few times each year to a house she felt was more desirable than the last made it difficult for Scott to establish friendships. And the Fitzgerald household was considered strange and forbidding by their neighbors, who saw a resemblance between the witch's-hat turret on one of their houses and the appearance of Mrs. Fitzgerald, a witchlike woman who carried an umbrella in all kinds of weather. Scott was already "desperately unpopular" at camp, an experience which would be repeated through his prep-school career, and he blamed his social failures on his mother, who, with her spoiling and pushing him, had ruined his chances for easy relationships with his peers. To be fair, it must be said that Fitzgerald's habit of sizing up people even as a small boy, an aptitude he would develop and turn to profitable use as a writer, infuriated his friends.

Money apparently was an important concern in the Fitzgerald family. Here he asks his mother for a dollar to put him on an equal footing with the other boys; and in answer to what must have been a similar request, his father wrote a few years later, "I enclose $1.00. Spend it liberally, generously, carefully, judiciously, sensibly. Get from it pleasure, wisdom, health, and experience." [15] That is a tall order for a child and a great deal to hope for from a piece of currency, but money was not easily come by for Edward Fitzgerald, who worked long but unprofitable hours as a salesman, a job which this retiring man must have found uncongenial. To escape the painful reality of his business failures and the censure of his ambitious wife, as Fitzgerald recorded in his Ledger, "His father used to drink too much and then play baseball in the backyard" (160). The drinking seems to have been an innocuous thing; it was a steady but quiet vice which hurt no one, and his father's inability to be dramatic in any way is congruent with the model of masculine failure he represented for Fitzgerald. He was, however, an actor in a drama which was a crucial one for Fitzgerald all of his days. He recorded the event in a March 1908 entry in his Ledger: "His father's services were no longer required by Procter and Gamble. He remembered the day, and that he gave his mother back his swimming money after he heard her at the phone." (162). In a 1936 interview,[16] in which he described this incident as the beginning of his father's life of failure, Fitzgerald revealed the depth to which it impressed him and the way he saw his father thereafter. Surely Fitzgerald's fictive impulse made him dramatize this incident and telescope all of the years of his father's failure into that one moment. Although he did not understand the substance of his mother's words, still he was conditioned to expect a disaster, and his immediate response was to return the quarter he had been given to spend and to pray that they would not be sent to the poorhouse. That quarter thus became a symbol of his father's loss of purpose and vitality. Not having had a penny for the collection box had meant acute embarrassment before a girl, and then this quarter became entangled in his imagination with the meaning of failure. Money meant social assurance, vitality, respectability; its absence or loss meant the disaster of the poorhouse or a kind of subtle undermining of one's vital energy and purpose. It is not surprising that the getting and spending of money was a major preoccupation of Fitzgerald's life and work.

A few months after his father lost his job, and with Scott now the male hope of the family, the Fitzgeralds returned to St. Paul, the seat of the McQuillan resources and vitality. The Fitzgeralds lived in the McQuillans' Victorian mansion for a year after their return to St. Paul, and for the first time Fitzgerald knew some stability in his living arrangements. Even when Mollie Fitzgerald resumed her nomadic habit, the McQuillan house remained a base for Scott. At least his mother's wanderings were restricted to one neighborhood, the Summit Avenue area where wealthy Catholic families had settled, but the Fitzgeralds were always just on the fringes of this affluent society. As he explained it in a letter to a friend at Smith College, which he headed "1st Epistle of St. Scott to the Smithsonian," the family always managed to find themselves "In a house below the average/Of a street above the average." [17]

The transiency of his early days would continue into his adulthood; he never owned a house or established a permanent residence anywhere, and his sense of rootlessness and desire for permanency are shared by most of his fictional characters. Amory Blain refuses to sell his family estate although he needs money desperately. Old Adam Patch's estate is the scene of the wedding of Anthony and Gloria, but they live in rented apartments and houses. Gatsby is unable to find the sense of tradition and stability he seeks in his "ancestral" mansion built by a brewer who had wanted to establish a baronial manor, and Nick Carraway rejects the transient life of the East for the Middle West where houses are called for decades by a family's name. Dick Diver is unable to reestablish himself in his father's country; the last thing we hear of him is that, after his return to upper New York State, he is probably in that section of the country "in one town or another." Monroe Stahr is building a house, but the landscape is supplied by the scenic technicians from his studio, and he will die before the contruction is finished. The lack of a sense of place in his boyhood affected Fitzgerald's own life and the lives of his fictional brothers.

The McQuillans had capital sufficient to support Mollie Fitzgerald's two spinster sisters and to give backing to her two brothers and herself. On the other hand, Edward Fitzgerald was little more than tolerated by the McQuillans, who had managed to get him a job as a wholesale grocery salesman which produced just enough money to pay for the corner he occupied of his brother-in-law's real estate office. Scott was humiliated by such indignities in the face of the McQuillan affluence and condescension. He loved his father, who had taught him gallantry ("When you enter a room speak first to the oldest lady, says father" [18]) and who had introduced him to the poetry of the Romantics, Poe and Byron. His father backed Fitzgerald in his ambition for a literary career against the McQuillans, who distrusted such impracticality and probably feared that, following such a course, he would repeat his father's failures. Mollie Fitzgerald went so far as to destroy most of what Scott wrote as a boy to influence his choice of a career, and he never forgave her insensitivity.[19] Fitzgerald suffered for his father whenever his mother said, "If it wasn't for Grandfather McQuillan where would we be now?" [20] but he also reluctantly recognized the truth of what she said.

The success of P. F. McQuillan was one of the most important elements of his background; in St. Paul and later at Newman and Princeton it was more useful to him than his father's aristocratic but exhausted Maryland lineage. But while Fitzgerald acknowledged the fact that his own vitality and ambition had descended to him through his mother, he never fully resolved his ambivalence toward her. Fitzgerald always used his father's standards as a moral touchstone (". . . always deep in my subconscious I have referred judgments back to him, what he would have thought, or done" [21]), and they pointed up the limitations of materialism. He recognized the nobility of his father's highest good, courtesy and the romance of the past and lost causes, and an essential part of him always yearned toward this, but the McQuillan vitality in him won out in the end. Yet Fitzgerald was aware of life's injustice to his father and others like him. "My father and Oscar Wilde born in the same year. One ruined at forty-one, one 'happy' at seventy. So Becky and Amelia are, in fact, *true.*" [22]

In his story "Shadow Laurels" (1915),[23] Fitzgerald tried to set right for himself the image of his father. His counterpart, Jacques Chandelle, returns to Paris to learn something about his dead father, a lazy little man whom his son remembers only for his having taught him to read and write. In spite of his opinion that his father had been an idler and a bad parent, still Jacques wants to know him. At the wine shop his father had frequented, Jacques learns that he had been attractive, a wonderful talker, poet, and singer, and that his friends felt he had expressed the best of them. His father becomes for Jacques "a poet unsinging," a father worthy to be his own. Before he leaves the shop where he has been drinking with his father's cronies, Jacques begins to assume the dead man's physical appearance ("His face is a little red and his hand unsteady. He appears infinitely more gallic than when he entered the wine shop" [77]), and the old men address him in their drunken stupor as the elder Chandelle. The good in his father's character now overshadows his former negative image, and Jacques has established a rapport with his heritage. The stories of other fathers and sons do not end so happily in Fitzgerald's work, for the sons ultimately learn that their fathers' legacies are inadequate equipment for success. But here for a time Fitzgerald found a congenial way in which to view his father.

With Edward Fitzgerald now a universally acknowledged failure, Mollie McQuillan assumed the major influence in Scott's life, and women dominated his life from this time on. His grandmother, whose major concern after her family was the Church, was a strong religious presence in his life. After her death, her daughter, Annabel, assumed the matriarchal role, and she, like her mother before her, played an active role in the Catholic life of St. Paul. Monsignor Louis Caillet, the pastor of St. Mary's Church which her father helped to build, and one of the first priests in the city, bequeathed to her a painting of a Madonna given to him by

James J. Hill "as a token of affection to her and of gratitude and friendship to her dear father and mother." [24] Aunt Annabel strongly influenced the decision to send Fitzgerald to the Newman School and probably paid the bills. She was a formidable person, and, while Fitzgerald did not feel warm affection for her, still he respected this woman whom he called the real matriarch of his family. A few months before he died Fitzgerald wrote that he was fond of her, for she gave him his first taste of discipline, in a way in which he was not fond of his mother, who spoiled him. Fitzgerald kept a picture of her in one of his scrapbooks; it shows a slender, unsmiling woman wearing a long black dress. Her hands are tightly, almost nervously, clasped before her, and her face is in shadows. In his list of story ideas in his "Notebooks," he included "Story of the ugly aunt in album."

When the Fitzgeralds returned to St. Paul, Scott was enrolled at St. Paul Academy, a nonsectarian prep school that had been established in 1900. No longer was there catechism instruction at school, but the McQuillan household was hardly free of religious influence. Annabel and her sister were devout Catholics who attended daily mass dressed in black, and who took Scott often to the Visitation Convent to declaim something he had written for the nuns. Furthermore, Ledger entries in the year 1910 indicate continued Catholic influence and activity in Scott's life. In January he noted, "Praying. Saving up Now I Lay Me's"; and in April, "Tried to go to St. Mary's Sunday School. Went to Father Busch instead. Became desperately Holy" (164).[25]

Fitzgerald's observation that he "became desperately holy" at age fourteen is an anomalous one. The onset of holiness in Catholic children usually comes three to four years earlier when the imitative phase of development begins in earnest and girls dress like nuns and boys talk of becoming priests while they begin to learn the Latin responses of the mass which an altar boy is required to know. The "Thoughtbook," a fourteen-page fragment of what was probably a much larger journal, which includes entries for 1910-11, indicates that the "desperately holy" Fitzgerald had not given his life over to asceticism, for its focus is his popularity with girls. The Fitzgerald of the "Thoughtbook" is desperately preoccupied with being first boy with the first girls, and we have seen in

"That Kind of Party" that he was interested in sex. Of course, holiness and sexuality are not mutually exclusive, just as the entries in the Ledger and the "Thoughtbook" do not present an irreconcilable contradiction. The important point is that Catholicism was an integral part of Fitzgerald's boyhood. Fitzgerald demonstrated, too, that he could be playfully irreverent. During communion at mass he saw that an altar boy was holding a candle dangerously close to the surplice of another acolyte, and Scott and a friend were ejected from the church because of their loud laughter. Apparently he used his incipient dramatic talent in all sorts of situations, for "his cousins . . . used to talk with amused tolerance (they were good Catholics) about how theatrically and superficially (as they thought) anti-Catholic FSF was as a small boy even." [26]

A May 1910 Ledger entry begins "Made 1st Communion" (164). Fitzgerald surely meant to say that he was confirmed in 1910, when he was fourteen, the customary age for this sacrament. If three years earlier he had lied in Confession, then he had already received Communion, for the two sacraments must go together. One is not allowed the sacrament of Confession if he has not demonstrated that he has memorized part of the catechism and that he understands the most elementary tenets of his religion. Fitzgerald must have gone through this much earlier than 1910, for the nuns who had been his teachers would never have allowed him to be unchurched. There are no records of Confirmations in the years 1905-16 at the St. Paul Cathedral; they have either been lost or no records were kept in that time.[27] From all the evidence, however, one must conclude that Fitzgerald was confirmed in St. Paul in or around 1910. He would not have been allowed to serve mass at the Newman School, and there is even some question if an officer of St. Patrick's Cathedral in New York would have officiated at the Fitzgeralds' marriage if he had not been confirmed.

A word on the composition of the Ledger might clarify Fitzgerald's error of substituting the word "Communion" for "Confirmation." The Ledger consists of three sections: an account of his earnings through 1936; a detailed record of his writings and their disposition, that is, whether or not they were published or if they were merely stripped of good passages and usable incidents, and their sales and royalties; and an irregular, fragmentary autobiographical chronology. In his introduction to the facsimile publication of the "Thoughtbook," John Kuehl says that Fitzgerald began to write the Ledger in the summer of 1922 and that it is probably indebted for information to the "Thoughtbook" and the lost larger journal.[28] The tone of the early entries in the Ledger clearly is detached and ironic.

> 1897   Dec.   Bronchitis. A specialist was summoned but as his advice was not followed the child pulled through
> 1900   Feb.   He celebrated the new century by swallowing a penny and catching the measles. He got rid of both of them. (154)

The Ledger entries which are coincident with the lost journal, however, seem to be very close to what must have been the substance and tone of that time. It is intriguing not only that the adolescent Fitzgerald recorded his Catholicism, possibly in the original "Thoughtbook" source, but also that the twenty-six-year-old Fitzgerald in 1922 recorded it for what he, in the egoism and energy of his extraordinary success, was sure was posterity.

For a full understanding of Fitzgerald's formative experiences, one must examine the character of the city of St. Paul, for what roots he had were here, and he returned to it for extended periods well into his adulthood. The town which Fitzgerald described in its early days as "a great fish just hauled out of the Mississippi and still leaping and squirming on its bank"[29] was and still is a decidedly Catholic town. After being opened up by Scandinavian explorers, the Minnesota Territory was founded by French Catholic missionaries in the late seventeenth century, and it was part of the Diocese of Quebec until the next century. St. Paul grew from a small trading post on the Mississippi to a major stepping-off point in the western exploration and the search for a route to the Pacific Ocean which was an obsession of the early French explorers.[30] Irish Catholic influence began in St. Paul in 1790, when John Carroll became bishop of Baltimore, a diocese which included all of the settled portions of the country. Frenchmen continued to govern the Minnesota Territory, however, with the assistance of immigrant Irish priests until Thomas Grace was installed as bishop of St. Paul in 1859, when Irish domination was finally institutionalized. The minority French presence had never been the genteel continentalism that took hold in New Orleans after French Catholics settled there. The long and harsh Minnesota winters and the rough frontier experience were not conducive to the sort of milieu established in New Orleans, and the influence of the Irish clergy drawn from the peasant class rather than from the intelligentsia of France prevailed in St. Paul.

Irish emigration to the city was promoted in the nineteenth century by the Minnesota Emigration Society, headed by Father John Ireland, who was to become the first archbishop of St. Paul in 1875 and a great national and international figure. Circulars were issued to Irish immigrants in the East encouraging them to move west, and by 1884 there were over 130,000 Catholics in St. Paul, the overwhelming majority of the population, and most of them were Irish,[31] But even though the Catholic majority was Irish, it was the older families of French Catholic lineage who were the aristocracy of the city, the principle of seniority having elevated them to that status. By 1908, the year in which the Fitzgeralds settled in St. Paul, it was a city of close to 200,000, approximately two-thirds of them Catholic. Its two foremost citizens were James J. Hill, builder of the Northern Railway, and Archbishop John Ireland, the builder of a great Catholic diocese, both of whom remained presences in Fitzgerald's life thereafter. Though Hill was not a Catholic, his wife and children were, and he and the Church established a symbiotic relationship. Hill built the Visitation Convent and Academy, St. Paul Seminary, and contributed much to the building of the cathedral in payment, as it were, for Bishop Grace's and Archbishop Ireland's provision of immigrant settlers, who in turn provided manpower and revenue for railroads to the coast.[32] Archbishop Ireland's cathedral dominates the city both physically and spiritually. Fitzgerald lived in its shadow, and in his description of it in his "Notebooks" in which he speaks of it as an immense white bulldog squatting on its haunches, he reveals a marked emotional bias. He noted and perhaps resented the bulldog tenacity of the institution it represents, but he surely never escaped its surveillance.

The residual effect of the rigid social structure of St. Paul is apparent in the Basil stories, "The Ice Palace," and in Nick Carraway's remarks and attitudes. The "best people" in St. Paul were Catholic, but not Irish Catholic, and this fact reinforced the social self-consciousness Fitzgerald had endured all of his short life. As if to discount the importance of his Irishness, as a young man he wrote to Edmund Wilson, who had included it with the Midwest and liquor as the significant influences on Fitzgerald in his 1922 *Bookman* article, "incidentally . . . I'm not Irish on Father's side—that's where Francis Scott Key comes in." [33] But Fitzgerald also noted that "As Tarkington says, American children belong to their mother's families," [34] and he was "Mollie McQuillan's boy," a fact that caused him much ambivalence and anguish.

It is questionable whether Fitzgerald ever made a satisfactory accommodation to his Irish Catholicism. Years later, always the self-conscious and resentful outsider, Fitzgerald recalled his boyhood friends' reaction to the strangeness of his religion: "When I was young," he said, "the boys in my street still thought that Catholics drilled in the cellar every night with the idea of making Pius the Ninth autocrat of the republic." [35] As a boy in St. Paul, at Newman, and at Princeton, a stronghold of the eastern Protestant upper class, his Catholic background was a large part of his sense of exclusion, and he fought hard to hide and forget it when he went east. It was not until Monsignor Fay and Shane Leslie, and Edmund Wilson opened up to him, respectively, a romantic and literary sort of Irish heritage that he would begin to speak with pride of his own Celtic background. Fay and Leslie suggested that Ireland was a romantic lost cause and that the Irish are charming people. These men knew about Celtic music and literature, and the priest had received a dispensation to say mass in Celtic. Although Fitzgerald, either through the influence of his provincial family or his teachers at the Newman School, had been made to believe that Joyce was a common Irishman outside the bounds of good taste, his mind was somewhat changed by Wilson's 1922 review of *Ulysses*. Furthermore, Wilson tried to convince Fitzgerald that there was a close connection between the milieu of *Ulysses* and

Fitzgerald's Irish Catholic and social background. But this romance and tenuous literary identification would fade with the death of Fay, the return of Leslie to England, and Fitzgerald's abandonment of Joycean subject matter after *This Side of Paradise* and "Absolution."

Fitzgerald explained his deepest feelings about being Irish and their social consequences in a 1933 letter to John O'Hara in which he discussed the intense social self-consciousness he shared with most of the Irishmen he knew. Even though he belonged to one of the most exclusive of the Princeton eating clubs, when in the most provincial place he would be intimidated by its social system and feel the necessity to justify himself. Just as his Catholic training had etched a profound morality in him that is the foundation of all of his serious work, so the fact of his being Irish in St. Paul and at prep school and college, his having moved from his lace-curtain Irish background into a larger society, gave him insight into the situation of the outsider in the world of the socially secure. He had been depressed by reading in Joyce's works of the struggle of the Irish bourgeoisie to rise above the drabness and lack of style of its life; *Ulysses* had given him a "hollow, cheerless pain" and made him feel "appallingly naked."

But whether Joyce's or Fitzgerald's characters ultimately have more hope is an open question. The inevitability of failure is an essential part of Fitzgerald's world view, and in his work, under the appearance of fashionable characters, glamorous situations, and an often lush style is a seriousness and morally critical view not often associated with the boy-wonder laureate of the Jazz Age. Fitzgerald, the first Irish Catholic to become a major American novelist, never allowed his religion and ancestry to become part of his public image; consequently they have not often been considered essential parts of his nature and work. Fitzgerald saw the Church as an Irish-American institution, provincial and unfashionable, a church for red-faced immigrant priests and serving girls with burlesque brogues— "The scullery maid of Christendom," as Joyce called it—and he was loath to be identified with this image. Yet his Irishness was an essential part of him, and the important theme of the heartbreak and moral failure which are inevitable for the parvenu and the awareness of the corruption of materialism in his best work could not have been but for his "straight 1850 potato famine Irish" background.

"A Night at the Fair," which is set in St. Paul in the summer before Basil goes east to prep school, is the best evidence we have of what Fitzgerald was like at fifteen. We see that Basil is "Alice Reilly's boy," the grandson of a "pioneer wholesale grocer," that his father is dead, as Fitzgerald's father was figuratively dead to him, and that he is financially dependent upon his mother's family. Basil's relationships with his peers are guarded and unsure, and he is aware of his social inferiority. Basil is squeamish and puritanical, and the *femme fatale* to whom he is attracted, his social and economic superior, teaches him a bitter lesson about his own inadequacy. In short, all of the formative influences that have been cited in Fitzgerald's boyhood are also operating in Basil's life. "A Night at the Fair" [36] was based upon an incident recorded in the September 1911 Ledger entry: "Attended State fair and took chicken on roller-coaster" (166). Aside from its importance to Fitzgerald, over fifteen years later he chose to record and characterize the onset of his young manhood with this experience, this incident probably was germinal in the development of the recurring metaphor in his work in which the amusement park, carnival, or world's fair is the vehicle, and corruption, sin, or sexuality is the tenor, his stylistic projection of the Augustinian City of Man.

This summer is a time of transition for Basil, and in the course of the story he acquires his first pair of long pants, a badge of manhood which all of his friends have already been awarded, and his first knowledge of the dangers involved in associations with women. Basil is with his friend, Riply Buckner, at the fair in the afternoon, and he is excited by the variety of experiences here—the exhibits of farming machinery, horse and auto races, "and a whining, tinkling hoochie-coochie show" (15), which at this point holds no particular significance for him. The boys see a "baby-faced" girl in a Blatz Wildcat with the aptly named Speed Paxton, and they wonder momentarily at this mystery; but this prefiguration of the other females in the story rides off, and what he has seen remains insignificant for Basil. His innocence is doomed, however, as the boys meet Elwood Leaming, who suggest that they "pick something up," and this is soon accomplished. The three boys and two girls, Basil still in his short pants the odd one, go off to the Old Mill, the tunnel-of-love ride. They move into the darkness, and the only sound Basil hears is his own boyish yelling while the others are involved in that mystery he has yet to experience. The amusement park suddenly becomes a hellish nightmare for Basil: "They slid into a red glow—a stage set of hell, with grinning demons and lurid paper fires—he made out that Elwood and his girl sat cheek to cheek—then again into the darkness" (20).

Basil abruptly leaves the others, and at home, titillated by what he has seen, he starts his campaign for the long pants he hopes will make him eligible to participate in the mystery. He gets the pants and arranges to meet the others the next night at the fair. Now in the darkness the fair has changed; only forms and shadows remain, and outlined in lights they suggest things "more mysterious and entrancing than themselves" (26). This is the sort of language that Father Schwartz uses in "Absolution" to describe the amusement park; the image that dominates his madness is the symbol of the "heat and the sweat and the life" that Rudolph Miller must observe from a distance in a dark place. But Basil is determined to face the mystery; he cannot remain detached. Up close he sees that his "chicken" is a masked woman; she has a "bad complexion brooding behind a mask of cheap pink powder and a shapeless mouth that tried ceaselessly to torture itself into the mold of charm" (26). They ride on the Ferris wheel, Father Schwartz's "big wheel made of lights," and the "chicken" encourages Basil to kiss her. He is stirred by it, but out of the corner of his eye he sees her masked face, and he is thankful when their car settles slowly to the ground. When Basil's archrival, Hubert Blair, arrives, Basil gladly slips away, leaving the other boys to contend with the predator.

Basil goes off to the fireworks and is asked to join the rich Golden Girl, Gladys Van Schellinger, and her parents in their box. His triumph is complete when the spectacle of "a short but monstrous procession, a sort of Lilliputian burlesque of the wild gay life" (29), his three friends and their questionable companions, passes before them. Basil is safe in respectability with the Golden

Girl, and his friends, consorting with this inferior sort of girl and having been seen by the adults in the box, face the prospect of their parents' censure. Later in the Van Schellinger limousine, suddenly in love with Gladys, Basil's triumph is at its crest when she asks him to visit her the next day. Supposedly as an afterthought she asks Basil to bring with him Hubert Blair, the leader of the parade. Basil had been deceived by Gladys's apparent innocence, "that vague unexciting quality" he had noted in her. On the other hand, Gladys recognizes in him a lack of daring, his holding himself back from sexual encounter, for the "exquisite delicacy" he thought he saw in her is actually his own. This is Basil's first lesson in the duplicity of Woman, and it is an experience that will occur again and again for him and for Fitzgerald's adult heroes. Basil's sexual fastidiousness and his association of sex with a vision of damnation in the hell-mouth of the Old Mill are probably the result of a combination of especially repressive moral training, for "Alice Reilly's boy" Catholic training, and his being raised in a home without a father. On the other hand, it is not certain that the model for Alice Reilly, Mollie Fitzgerald, should bear the full responsibility of her son's lifelong fascination with the *femme fatale,* but it is probable that the model of the relationship of the sexes which she presented to him was profoundly influential.

The Buffalo and St. Paul years, the Catholic orientation and troubled family situation, left their mark on Fitzgerald as man and as artist. The attitudes, morality, values, and his impression of the nature of sexual relationships which were formed in this time he carried with him throughout his life, and they are the foundation of the themes and characterizations in his work.

Literary Apprenticeship: 1911-1917
The Newman School and Princeton

Fitzgerald's career at St. Paul Academy had been an uneven one; his English teacher encouraged him to write, and Fitzgerald followed his advice to a fault. Since he spent class time alternately working on his fiction behind propped-up books and irritating the other boys by arrogantly displaying his "suppressed knowledge," he was disliked by both students and teachers. In fact, an anonymous writer in the school magazine once requested that someone "poison young Scottie or find a means to shut his mouth." [37] Fitzgerald recognized that sports might be a way to achieve popularity, but he was small and not well coordinated. He had a few dramatically heroic moments on the football field, and he wore his several injuries as badges, but his distinction was to lie elsewhere. In his last two years at St. Paul's, the school magazine published four of his stories, and his future course was set.

But Fitzgerald's family were concerned about his poor grades and his preoccupation with his writing which they, with the exception of his father, hoped to discourage. They felt that a fresh start at some distant boarding school and the discipline that would be enforced there would straighten him out. A family council was held, and Aunt Annabel agreed to bear the expense of his prep-school education, provided it was a good Catholic school. [38] In the fall of 1911, an excited and expectant young Fitzgerald went east primed for adventure, even though he was a bit disappointed that he was not going to an older established school. When someone told him that he had never heard of Newman, Fitzgerald answered rather defensively, "It's a good school—you see, it's a *Catholic* school." [39]

The Newman School was founded in 1900 by Catholic laypeople, the Bostonians Dr. and Mrs. Jesse A. Locke. Before Locke's conversion to Catholicism, he had been an Episcopal priest and had taught at some fine Episcopal schools. Mrs. Locke was a niece of Isaac Thomas Hecker, [40] a controversial figure in the history of the American Catholic Church. At the suggestion of his friend Orestes Brownson, as a young man Hecker spent some time at Brook Farm. Later he lived with the Thoreau family in Concord, but the extreme individualism of Transcendentalism was not the solution to his spiritual questing. He became a Catholic (his attempts to convert Thoreau were unsuccessful), joined the Redemptorist Missionary order, and in 1858 founded the Missionary Priests of St. Paul the Apostle in New York. Hecker, for his time, was a bit of an activist, for he saw the Church as essentially a democratic institution, a view which brought him some enmity from within the ranks. He was charged with trying to establish an independent American Catholic Church, a charge he vehemently denied.[41]

Locke's intention was to create a school that would "equal the best college preparatory schools in the country on the scholastic side" [42] and to offer the religious and moral training he felt secular schools did not provide. In fact, Locke hoped to create a school which would rival the excellence of Eton, and, to evoke associations with the prestigious English public schools, he named it for the English cardinal John Henry Newman. In some respects Newman was modeled after the Oratory School founded by Cardinal Newman in England in 1859.[43] Its curriculum apparently emphasized classical education,[44] and Newman was unique among American Catholic schools in that, like its English model, it was administered by laymen and its teaching staff were permitted to marry.

The channels of the Church's association with Newman have been difficult to trace; the records of the school have vanished, and a search of various diocesan archives has yielded no information. Apparently the school was founded in 1900 under the patronage or with the unoffical approval of John Cardinal Farley,[45] who was then president of the Catholic School Board of the New York Diocese.[46] By 1911, the year Fitzgerald entered, the Newman School had moved from its first quarters in Dr. Locke's home in Orange, New Jersey, to the Hackensack campus, where it remained until 1920, when it moved to Lakewood, New Jersey. Dr. Locke's dream of establishing "a select preparatory school for the sons of prominent Roman Catholic families" [47] unfulfilled, Newman ceased operations in 1941, when its trustees decided that its future was too bleak to warrant its continued operation.[48]

While the school was located in the Diocese of Newark, although it apparently had no formal association with his diocese, the bishop of Newark, John J. O'Connor, lent his official presence to school ceremonies. He blessed the school's new chapel at the 1913 graduation exercises.[49] In 1914 a clergyman of still another diocese made clear his association with Newman. Cardinal Gibbons of Baltimore, the patron of Monsignor Fay, visited the school on his way to Rome, an important event in the school's brief history. Gibbons, who had "always displayed a keen interest in Newman,"[50] was driven to the school in the car of John G. Agar, president of the board of trustees, a prominent New York lawyer who also served as a trustee of Catholic University and on the boards of several large corporations, the father of a star Newman athlete. The octogenarian cardinal was welcomed in Latin by a prominent Newmanite, Joseph Porter Toole, grandson of the first governor of Montana. Gibbons's address to the school body, a rousing apology for exclusive Catholic education, was enthusiastically received by the boys, who sent him off with a spirited school yell.[51]

The school had begun in 1900 with only four students; in 1901 there were fourteen, in 1902 twenty, and in 1911 Fitzgerald was one of sixty boys. The following year Newman was merged with the Hume School of New Rochelle, New York, which had been founded by Nelson Hume, an assistant master and drama coach at Newman eight years before, who, with the merger, became associate headmaster of the Hackensack school.[52] In the fall of 1912, there were seventy-five boys registered, and the facilities were overtaxed, for another building had to be rented to accommodate them.[53] Newman was located on the fourteen-acre country estate of Frank W. Poor on both sides of Essex Street, an area of Hackensack rich in the lore of the Revolutionary War. It is telling that even though the school was known for its strong faculty, they emphasized their athletic facilities and the fact that they encouraged outdoor sports; their description of the school, written for a directory, failed to mention the curriculum.[54] Newman fielded football, hockey, basketball, baseball, and soccer teams, and in their full athletic schedule they competed against public schools in the area as well as private schools in New Jersey, New York, and Connecticut.

Newman's rivalry with Hackensack High School was especially fierce and was not restricted to athletic contests. A group of Newmanites, whom the townspeople thought were "too proud," went into town each Saturday night to challenge their Hackensack counterparts for the possession of the corner of Main and Mercer streets, the site of a popular confectionery. The first group to arrive claimed it and held off the usurpers from the rival school.[55] This ritual was typical of Newmanite behavior. The academic and personal discipline that Fitzgerald's family had wanted for him was not likely to be imposed by a staff that was frequently cowed by its students. The Newman of Fitzgerald's day has been compared with Clongowes Wood, the Jesuit school outside Dublin attended by James Joyce, where students were just as interested in rebelling as the Newmanites, who staged sit-down strikes, went to a neighboring roadhouse to drink beer, and in general defied the school's rule with gusto.[56]

Fitzgerald's wealthy schoolmates came from all over the country, and not all of this largely Irish group were Catholics. Among the graduates of Newman was Frank Couzens, a Presbyterian, who later became mayor of Detroit like his father before him; and James Couzens, who was also a United States senator and vice president and treasurer of the Ford Motor Company. This association brought a major celebrity to the Newman campus in 1914, when Henry Ford visited Frank Couzens and his brother Homer, who were recuperating from the mumps.[57] Fitzgerald was not the only literary man who graduated from Newman. Although he did not reach Fitzgerald's eminence, Humphrey Cobb did make his mark with his popular antiwar novel *Paths of Glory*. Cobb was born in the home of the Brownings, Casa Guidi, in Florence, but his Boston parents came home to give their son an American education at the Newman School. In 1916, at the age of seventeen, Cobb enlisted in the Canadian army and was sent to France where he served through the end of World War I. He was wounded and was gassed twice and used this experience in writing his only novel.[58]

Fitzgerald's schoolmates at Newman reacted predictably to his boasting, his criticism of them, and his showing-off in class. It was St. Paul Academy all over again, but now without the favor of his home he was totally miserable. In "The Freshest Boy," [59] one of the Basil stories, Fitzgerald describes his first year at Newman. Within a few weeks he had been forced into several fistfights with the crowd against him, he was ostracized by masters and students alike, and was called either by the epithet "Bossy" or just his last name. His delicate good looks (four years later he received an embarrassing number of votes as the prettiest member of his Princeton class) quickly earned him a reputation as a sissy, and his general misery was compounded by his realization that "he was one of the poorest boys in a rich boy's school" (28).[60] Fitzgerald's escapes from the painful social situation at Newman were the solitude of his room ("Basil was snubbed and slighted a good deal for his real and imaginary sins, and he was much alone" [45]) and the New York theater, when he was not on bounds. In his Ledger, Fitzgerald called this time at Newman "a year of real unhappiness" (166); but it was also the shock that he needed to make him see life realistically, and he began then really to grow up. He was not changed overnight, however, for his indulgent mother had not given him good work habits, and most of his attempts to make a new start failed. His marks did improve slightly, and he won the junior field meet, but this did not appreciably increase his popularity. Escape would have been possible, but he was determined to stick it out, and almost all he had to show for his first year of adventure in the East was his perseverance in the face of universal loathing.

Back in St. Paul for the summer, Fitzgerald's friends saw a change in him, a sadness and apparently a new reticence. He found himself the favorite boy of the top girls, but the boys saw through him when he regressed and put them off with his bragging. His second year at Newman was better, but, as his Ledger indicates, it was not a total success: "Reward in the fall for work of previous summer. A better year but not happy" (167). The "work of previous summer" was some reading, but primarily writing, and back at Newman Fitzgerald's resolve to make his way as a writer was strengthened. He had failed ignominiously on the football field and had been taken out of a game by his coach, who thought Fitzgerald was yellow. He compensated for this disgrace by turning to the solitary creative act, and many years later in "Author's House" he recorded this incident among his formative experiences. He chose to work out the emotional impact of his disgrace in writing a poem for the school newspaper, which made as big a hit with his father as if he had become a football hero. He discovered then "a back door out of facing reality." that if he could not "function in action," at least he could tell about it because he "felt the same intensity." [61] He had become a writer.

Fitzgerald was writing stories, too, and three of them were published in the *Newman News*. "The Luckless Santa Claus" and "The Trail of the Duke" are mildly moralistic pieces in which a rather dim-witted young man is the dupe of a typical Fitzgerald female, a willful and spoiled destroyer. The third, "Pain and the Scientist," is a satirical view of Christian Science. However, just as his St. Paul Academy stories—an improbable and overplotted mystery, a wish-fulfilling anecdote of a football triumph, and two fanciful Civil War pieces—were highly imaginative and were based upon his reading rather than his own experience, so the Newman stories do not reflect the actual experience of that time. Fitzgerald was decidedly an autobiographical writer, but he most effectively used his experience several years after the fact when he had digested its significance.

Fitzgerald said that at fifteen, when he entered Newman, his puritan conscience made him think he was worse than most boys because of his latent unscrupulousness and the desire to influence people in some way, even for evil. This exaggerated statement of his moral condition is an instance of the underlying and sometimes burdensome Catholic conscience with which he came to Newman and which he would carry all his life. That the absolutism of his religion had made him set impossible standards for himself is clear in a 1915 Ledger entry: "My sense of perfection. If I couldn't be perfect I wouldn't be anything" (169). Fitzgerald was always too hard on himself; he wanted to be best at whatever he attempted, and perhaps when he realized that he could not be a perfect Catholic, he became extreme in his public renunciation of his religion, a pose he had assumed even in his boyhood in St. Paul.

This spiritual dilemma and its extreme resolution is the subject of "The Perfect Life" [62] in which Basil, for a time, becomes the conscience of St. Regis. Basil has finally won approval with his fine performance in a football game; and John Granby, an old graduate who is visiting the school, makes Basil realize that his new heroic status has given him the power to influence his schoolmates to lead "clean, upright, decent lives." For several weeks he buttonholes the more conspicuous sinners and talks to them "about swearing and smoking and writing home and a lot of stuff like that" (95). Basil's evangelism even extends to one of his friends' sister, Jobena Dorsey, who he is convinced will be damned by her wild behavior unless he saves her. Basil is attracted to her, but he remembers John Granby's admonition, "Every time you kiss a nice girl you may have started her on the road to the devil" (100). Basil tells her that she should not smoke, dance suggestively, and especially not kiss anyone but her family. Jobena finds him "a nasty little prig," and since the thought of marriage to someone like him repels her, she resolves to marry Skiddy DeVinci, a hard drinker who has been fired from Yale. Basil waylays him on the way to the elopement and compromises his own newfound and tentative moralism by manipulating Skiddy into a state of drunken insensibility. The three cocktails Basil has drunk have relaxed his principles, and Jobena now seems the most attractive girl he has ever known. After several kisses in a dark elevator, she approves of the real Basil beneath the pious mask and returns his affection. Basil goes back to school and his life of sin boasting of his fatal propensity for liquor and Jobena's concern for his future. His short priestly life ends when the advantages of vice over smug, false piety become clear to him.

Religious life at Newman was almost as relaxed as it was at Basil's St. Regis. The boys were required to attend mass only on Sundays and holy days of obligation, but Fitzgerald seemed relatively serious about his religion. He noted in his Ledger that in January 1912 he was ". . . serving Mass" (168), but his duties as an acolyte did not make him less whimsically irreverent, for he also noted that he "Gave up spinach for Lent." [63] Fitzgerald's grades at Newman were as erratic as his athletic performances. His fifth-form midyear report card shows that he failed Latin composition; just passed history, English, algebra, and geometry; did slightly better in English composition, French, and Latin; but he received a distinguished grade in his Christian doctrine course.[64]

Perhaps the most important event of Fitzgerald's time at Newman was his meeting Father Cyril Sigourney Webster Fay, a trustee of the school and its headmaster the year after Fitzgerald left. Fay was a charming, ebullient, eccentric, and altogether delightful phenomenon for Fitzgerald, who had never seen anyone quite like him. The corpulent albino with a high-pitched voice and shrill laughter presented a startling exterior. His contagious merriment, however, his wit (which he directed at himself as well as the Church), and, most important, his interest in and sympathy for Fitzgerald (who he saw was suffering even as Fay himself must have as a boy) won Fitzgerald over quickly.

Fay's background was a good deal more worldly and interesting than that of the other priests Fitzgerald had known. His mother, Susan Hutchinson Fay, was from a Philadelphia family that had been prominent in that city for almost two hundred years. The Bucks County and western New Jersey branches of the family comprised landed and wealthy farmers and merchants. The family was established in Philadelphia by Dr. James H. Hutchinson (1752-93), who was perhaps Father Fay's most interesting ancestor. He studied medicine at the then recently established University of Pennsylvania and, after further study in England, returned to America in 1777 by way of France, bringing with him dispatches from Benjamin Franklin to the Continental government. As his ship approached the coast, it was pursued by a British man-of-war and he landed under enemy fire. After this experience Dr. Hutchinson became an impassioned patriot dissatisfied with what he considered was the conservatism of the Continental government, and after his death was spoken of as an enemy by John Adams in a letter to Thomas Jefferson. Still Dr. Hutchinson enjoyed a cordial relationship with George Washington, who dined with him when he visited the city.

Hutchinson vigorously practiced medicine both during and after the Revolution. He was commissioned a surgeon in the Pennsylvania navy in 1778 and later became the director and physician general of the army hospitals in Pennsylvania, a member of the surgical staff of Pennsylvania Hospital, and a professor of chemistry at the University of Pennsylvania. Hutchinson was one of the founders of the Whig Association, which was formed to prevent associations with Tories "and other suspect persons." and he served as secretary of the American Philosophical Society and as a trustee of the University of Pennsylvania. Through his social activities he brought his family into association with members of the Rittenhouse, Wharton, and Girard families, the most prominent names in the city. Dr. Hutchinson died in 1793 of yellow fever contracted while he attended victims in the great epidemic of that year. The descendants of Dr. Hutchinson and Father Fay's maternal forebears further established the importance of the family in Philadelphia in the fields of commerce, medicine, and law. Several had been distinguished bankers, attorneys and judges, physicians, and professors and trustees of the University of Pennsylvania.[65]

Fay's father, Alfred Forbes Fay, was a Bostonian who married Susan Hutchinson in Philadelphia in 1869, when they were both twenty-seven, after four years of distinguished service in the Union Army. Fay enlisted on November 8, 1861, at the age of nineteen, as a private in the 30th Massachuseets Volunteers Infantry, as he said, "to help crush the Rebellion."[66] Just a week later he was promoted to commissary sergeant, his next promotion to second lieutenant coming in October 1862, awarded for bravery in the Battle of Baton Rouge where he commanded a company and was shot in the knee. Between 1862 and 1864 Fay also fought at the taking of New Orleans, in all the battles of the lower Mississippi campaign, at Vicksburg, Port Hudson, and with the Army of the Potomac.[67] In May 1864, Fay resigned his commission to reenlist as a captain in the 1st United States Volunteer Infantry (Enlisted Prisoners of War), although his rank was listed as "Acting Major." He was mustered in at Norfolk, Virginia, for a three-year tour and six months later was sent to Fort Rice in the Dakota Territory to fight Indians. He submitted his resignation in June of that year because "the Rebellion [was] over and family matters [needed] his attention at home."[68] In October 1865, then holding the rank of captain, Fay was honorably discharged for physical disability. (Since he later used the title of "Brevet Lt. Colonel," his disability pension probably was considerably larger than the amount paid a regular army captain.) Aside from the gunshot wound he received at Baton Rouge, Captain Fay suffered greatly from other service-related ailments. The doctor's testimonial of his disability mentions an inguinal hernia cause by a fall in 1865, and apparently he developed rheumatism and scurvy that year "from want of vegetables in the Dakotah Territory."[69]

When Captain Fay died as a result of these afflictions in 1881 at the age of thirty-nine, he left his widow with two children, their six-year-old son named for his father's brother, Sigourney Webster

Fay, an attorney of New York, and a four-year-old daughter, Mary Forbes Fay. Mrs. Fay survived her son by several years; she died in Asbury Park, New Jersey, in 1926 at the age of eighty-four.[70]

Fay's family background paralleled Fitzgerald's in that it was his mother and her family who were prominent in the city where they lived and who provided him with a firm social and financial base, while it was his father who must have been considered an outsider. Moreover, it is curious that Monsignor Fay should have adopted as one of his favorite romantic lost causes the plight of the South; it would seem more likely for him to have been attracted by the romantic memory of his father, a martyr to the Union cause.

After his graduation from the University of Pennsylvania in 1897, Fay attended the Episcopal Divinity School in Philadelphia. He had always had High Church leanings, and he was ordained an Episcopal priest in 1903 at Fond du Lac, Wisconsin, where he had gone because of its Catholic reputation. He was archdeacon at Fond du Lac before he went to Nashotah House, an Episcopal seminary located outside Milwaukee, to teach dogma and moral theology. There he joined the Companions of the Holy Savior, a group of Anglican clergy who wanted to institutionalize the influence of the English Oxford Movement. They conducted private daily masses for each priest almost totally according to the Roman rite, used both the Book of Common Prayer and the Roman breviary, eucharistic vestments, Gregorian chant, and incense. They stressed meditation and vespers, and generally tried to create a monastic atmosphere.[71] The General Convention of the Episcopal Church suspected that this group wanted to deliver them to Rome, and they took measures to restrict the activities of the Companions. In 1908, the year of Fay's conversion to Catholicism, he was given an indefinite leave of absence from his duties at Nashotah after several students and two priests from Nashotah House left the Anglican for the Roman Catholic church. What affected Fay's final decision seems to have been the Pope's condemnation of modernism, upon which Fay stated publicly, "We must obey the Holy Father." [72] He was received into the Church at Deal, an exclusive community on the New Jersey shore where his mother kept a summer home. After two more years of study, he was ordained a Catholic priest by Cardinal Gibbons in

Baltimore.[73] He became a favorite and confidant of Cardinal Gibbons and soon launched his career as a much sought after preacher and as a society priest, a rarity among American clergy.

Mrs. Winthrop Chanler, whom Fitzgerald met through Fay and used as the model for Mrs. Lawrence in *This Side of Paradise*, describes her family's unique relationship with Father Fay in her memoir, *Autumn in the Valley*. She had spent much time in Europe; her family owned a home at Newport; and her eighth and last child was named for Theodore Roosevelt who, with Mrs. Cabot Lodge, sponsored the child at his christening.[74] She built her Chapel of St. Felicitas on her Hudson River estate, and she received permission from Rome to reserve the consecrated elements of communion, and for biweekly mass, weddings, and funerals to be celebrated there.[75]

The Chanlers met Father Fay in Washington, and he was delighted by them and their European sort of Catholicism. He spent time with them each summer and every day observed prime, though the Chanler children often rebelled at this, and said daily mass. He also performed other, more unusual rites; with two of the boys acting as acolytes he blessed every room in the house, the stable and horses, and the gardens. He exorcised a plague of worms in the Chanlers' wheat fields and delighted the children with his playlets in which he played the Pope and one of the children, fitted out with pillows, played Fay. He entertained them with Irish songs and stories delivered in a burlesque brogue and conversations which he insisted be conducted in Latin, and he admonished them all that enjoying good food and drink was a way to praise. After he was made a monsignor, a rite Mrs. Chanler attended in Rome, he modeled for them his finery in which "he looked like nothing so much as an enormous peony floating about." [76] The Chanlers' was a mixed marriage, and they had agreed, under the jurisdiction of the Italian Church, which is not so rigid as the American Church in such matters, that their daughters be Catholics and their sons Episcopalians. Fay, in a secret irregularity, initiated two of the boys into Catholicism with the Sacrament of First Communion.

In his itinerant life as a preacher who was much in demand, Fay considered the Chanlers his parish, and he brought to them from Rome a relic of the True Cross, an honor usually reserved for bishops, and a Roman chasuble for the chapel. Even after his death Fay remained in spirit with the Chanlers as a resident saint, for Mrs. Chanler tells us that her children continued to pray to him for favors better-known saints might not be bothered with.[77]

Monsignor Fay was also a constant visitor with the Chanlers in the home of Henry Adams in Washington. Adams was deeply interested in twelfth- and thirteenth-century music, and he was introduced to Fay by his Catholic secretary, who knew of Fay's expertise on this subject. Adams was charmed by this "round, jolly, worldly" priest who helped to make his last years easier.[78] But Fay did not accomplish what must have been a fond wish, for Adams wrote: "Father Fay is no bore—far from it, but I think he has an idea that I want conversion, for he directs his talk much to me, and instructs me. Bless the genial sinner! He had best look out that I don't convert him. . . . "[79] Fay's associations with society figures led him to an interest in an historical counterpart of his. He was the founder and first president of the St. John Chrysostom Society,[80] an organization devoted to the study of the life and writing of the seventeenth-century Franciscan priest and a leading figure of the Norman mystics. Chrysostom was the confessor of Marie de Medici and Anne of Austria and was a favorite of Louis XIII and Cardinal Richelieu—a priest Fay would certainly wish to emulate.

Fay introduced Fitzgerald to a Catholicism he never knew existed; as Fitzgerald put it, "he made of that Church a dazzling, golden thing, dispelling its oppressive mugginess and giving the succession of days upon gray days, passing under its plaintive ritual, the romantic glamour of an adolescent dream." [81] Converts to Catholicism often are extremely zealous; Fay, who said that his conversion was a "bound into the arms of God" [82] and that he had found the romance of his life in the Church, was no exception. The urbane Fay sympathized with Fitzgerald's disdain for his provincial Irish Catholic background, and he hoped to show Fitzgerald the glamour of the Church and to infuse him with his own enthusiasm and childlike faith, and for several years he was successful. In fact, Father Fay supplanted Edward Fitzgerald in

Scott's life; this was a father who was a gourmet and connoisseur of wines, a perfumed dandy, a confidant of renowned churchmen who was befriended by literary and society figures.

Fay was not a first-rate intellect, however, as his published sermons, rife with sentimental theological metaphors and formulaic ideas, and the assessment of those who knew him early in his career, attest. He was "brilliant and unstable" and could change any opinion he held overnight; shortly before his conversion he had been working on a book to prove the invalidity of Roman orders.[83] But Fay was constant in his belief in the tenets of Catholicism and in his affection and concern for the young Fitzgerald, whom he wanted to save for the Church. Just as his own father had introduced Fitzgerald to the poetry of Poe and the romance of the South, so Fay influenced Fitzgerald's literary tastes by encouraging him to read the works of the fin de siècle poets and novelists Swinburne, Huysmans, Wilde, and the more orthodox Robert Hugh Benson. Fay also made Fitzgerald see the romantic possibilities of a glittering international Church patronized by a wealthy and aristocratic elite and the noble situation of the oppressed Irish. Fitzgerald was delighted to find the old religion and his Irish heritage not only suddenly acceptable but glamorous and attractive. Fitzgerald's friendship with Fay would grow and be most important after he had gone on to Princeton, but their initial meeting at Newman made it a slightly more pleasant place for him to be, and it would later qualify him as one of the privileged "old boys" remembered by Dr. Locke when he was sending out reproductions of a portrait of himself he had commissioned for the school.[84]

In the spring of his second year at Newman, Fitzgerald went to Norfolk to visit a member of his father's family, his favorite first cousin, Cecelia Taylor. The important event of this trip was his visit with her brother, Thomas Delihant, who was studying at the Jesuit seminary at Woodstock in Maryland. Just how deeply impressed Fitzgerald was by this visit he indicated in a 1924 magazine article in which he listed some of his heroes; in a catalogue that includes Theodore Roosevelt, Admiral Dewey, James J. Hill, and Garibaldi he included a "certain obscure Jesuit priest."[85] The only Jesuit he seems to have known was Thomas

Delihant. This visit would produce "The Ordeal" and "Benediction," two of Fitzgerald's few overtly Catholic pieces. Apparently the sixteen-year-old Fitzgerald's exposure to the special sort of tranquility of a religious community and to Tom Delihant at the time of his most momentous decision—he was about to take his final vows—deeply affected him. We cannot know if the character of the novice in "The Ordeal" and his spiritual crisis are accurate representations of Delihant and his state just before his ordination. Perhaps Fitzgerald built upon the hint of apprehension he must have seen in Delihant facing his life's decision, or perhaps Fitzgerald, who had chosen Father Fay as a model and was beginning to speculate about the priesthood for himself, was considering what his own feelings would be in this situation. Surely Delihant's ordination was not a precipitous affair, for the eighteen-year course of preparation for entry into the Society of Jesus is the longest and most rigorous of the Catholic orders.

Thomas Delihant grew up in the area and atmosphere that had produced Edward Fitzgerald's antebellum sensibility, a fact which must have figured in his attraction for Fitzgerald. Delihant was born in Chicago in 1878, and when he was thirteen came east with his family where he lived in Maryland for a time and then in Georgetown in Washington. He finished his sophomore year at Georgetown University, where Fitzgerald's father had studied, before at age nineteen he entered the Jesuit order at Frederick, Maryland. There he spent four years in the study of poetry, rhetoric, and philosophy before he was sent to teach mathematics at Holy Cross High School in Baltimore and at St. Joseph's College in Philadelphia. In 1909 he went to Woodstock, where he spent the next three years in his final theology course before his ordination to the priesthood by James Cardinal Gibbons in June 1912. Then he went on to teaching assignments at St. Andrew's in Poughkeepsie and at Loyola College in Baltimore. He took his final vows in 1914 and then spent one year as a service chaplain and three years on the Mission Band, a group of itinerant preachers who either serve areas where there is no parish priest or supplement the Sunday mass schedules of small churches. After a four-year stay in Baltimore as a parish priest, he went to his final assignment at St. Ignatius Church in New York City where he remained for twenty-one years before being retired to Inisfada on Long Island. Two years later he died after an extended illness and was buried at the novitiate in Wernersville, Pennsylvania.[86]

His was not an especially distinguished career; there is certainly nothing particularly heroic in the bare facts of Delihant's life to have recommended him to the company of Roosevelt and Garibaldi in Fitzgerald's pantheon. Probably his spirituality and gentleness, noted by all who knew him, most impressed a Fitzgerald fresh from the tutelage of Father Fay. The official Jesuit obituary-eulogy for Delihant written by an old friend and colleague reveals something of the character and personality of the man. It notes a predisposition to nervousness and headaches, an inability to concentrate and to acquire and coordinate knowledge, his ineptness with scholastic philosophy, and his distaste for teaching. That Delihant could remain a Jesuit with these liabilities is testimony to the strength of his positive qualities—his finely honed intuitive powers, his gift for getting close to all sorts of people, and his ability to move and engage people in his sermons. The very rich were his friends, a fact that impressed Fitzgerald, and he was an enthusiastic horseman and sailor when the indulgence of his wealthy friends allowed him to be. The novitiate at Wernersville was donated to the order by a wealthy layman who said he gave it to express his gratitude for Father Delihant's attention and service to his family. On the other hand, for the twenty years he worked in New York he was drawn to and absorbed by the problems of the very poor of his parish. He was possessed of the great humanness and sweetness of the priest Keith in "Benediction" that made him the good priest Fitzgerald admired.

Although he had been born in Chicago and his father was a born Irishman, the transplantation of the young Delihant in Maryland had taken well, and nurtured, he grew into a Dixie man of antebellum sentiments. He was proud of his kinship to Francis Scott Key, and he told a friend that when he meditated on heaven he imagined himself asked by General Lee to carry dispatches for him.[87] This romanticism and deep sympathy for the lost cause of the South were qualities Fitzgerald admired, and it is clear that he identified Delihant with those qualities of Edward Fitzgerald of which he was most fond and proud.

Two priests had profoundly affected Fitzgerald during his Newman years, but back in St. Paul to spend the summer before entering Princeton, his interest turned to more secular matters. Instead of studying to make up for his deficient grades at Newman, he wrote his second play for a local drama group. He was also preoccupied with financial problems, as we see in "Forging Ahead" in which Basil's mother's business losses threaten to sentence him to four years at the state university instead of his long-dreamed-of career at Yale. The analogue in Fitzgerald's life to this was his Aunt Annabel's wish for him to go to Catholic Georgetown and her refusal to pay his way at Princeton. Fitzgerald was adamant, however, and his family supported his decision, certainly with the full approval of Edward Fitzgerald, who must have liked the idea of his son's attending a southern gentleman's university. It is not clear if Aunt Annabel relented or if the Fitzgeralds bore the total expense, but somehow the money was found. But even after the resolution of this financial crisis, Fitzgerald's way to Princeton was not a smooth one. His Newman grades were deficient, and he was required to take makeup exams. They did not give him enough credits, however, so he appealed personally to the admissions committee, which he apparently charmed. His most persuasive arguing point was that the day of the interview was his birthday and it would be cruel to turn him down. Upon his acceptance he immediately wired his mother to send his football pads and shoes and to hold his trunk.

Fitzgerald loved Princeton from the first: its physical beauty, the intrigues of campus politics, the competition among the eating clubs, and the varieties of people and experiences it offered him. Surely he could find a place here away from the stultification of St. Paul, his Irish Catholic background, and the confinement of Newman. One's dress, the prep school one attended, and whether one was from the East or the West were extremely important social distinctions at Princeton in those days, and Fitzgerald quickly tried to adapt to what was acceptable; some thought he tried too hard and made himself conspicuous.[88] The liability of his midwestern background was somewhat neutralized by the fact that he had been east to school, but he was still a Catholic from an undistinguished prep school in a Protestant university, and he needed great public success in order to feel secure. He gave up football ostensibly because of an injury, but probably simply because he was outclassed; and he turned to the Triangle Club and the campus humor magazine, The Tiger, for his way to distinction. He graduated from working on lighting in his freshman year to writing the book and lyrics for the 1914 show, *Fie! Fie! Fi-Fi,* but he was ineligible throughout his time at Princeton, and he could not participate as an officer or actor in the club's productions. This way to acclaim blocked, he eventually began to write seriously for the *Nassau Literary Magazine,* in part because of the influence of John Peale Bishop, then a twenty-one-year-old freshman whom Fitzgerald respected for his seriousness about literature.

In June of his freshman year, the *Nassau Literary Magazine* published "The Ordeal," [89] which Fitzgerald had written after his visit with Father Delihant.[90] The story concerns a young novice who, in the hour before taking his vows, reviews the course of testing and decision-making which has brought him to this juncture; his secular education and foreign travel, the possibility of a career in law or the diplomatic service, the disappointment and disapproval of his family and friends, his prayer, and his final acceptance of his vocation. The singing of a group of black workers disturbs his meditation, and he is reminded of the comforts and diversions of his southern plantation home. Worldly visions march before his mind's eye: art, beauty, love; events and men which question the moral and philosophical rectitude of the church—the burning of Wycliffe, the treachery of Pope Alexander VI, the Inquisition, the skepticism of Huxley, Nietzsche, Zola, Kant, Voltaire, and Shaw. Watching the novice in his reverie are the "sweet sad eyes" of a woman who in the course of his visions becomes the masked destroyer: "The girl's eyes were all wrong, the lines around her mouth were cold and chiselled and her passion seemed dead and earthy"(84). His horror at her transformation and his prayer dispel this momentary temptation, and as the chapel bell tolls the hour of the ceremony, he returns to calm and resolve.

Kneeling in the chapel he notices an older fair-haired, green-eyed novice whose glance darts nervously around the chapel. Now, when a Fitzgerald character has green eyes he is either a counterpart of Fitzgerald or he/she represents some dimension of his experience or being. This nervous green-eyed novice is a correlative of Fitzgerald's skepticism and knowledge of evil, for after he has captured the protagonist's eye he directs his attention to the altar candle with his darting eyes. The apprehensions of the previous hour revisit the novice as he senses an evil presence in the chapel. A great weight presses down upon him, and he is momentarily transported to another dimension, where anomalously the sacred candle seems to contain the essence of evil. Here good is crushed under the cloven foot, evil palpably prevails, and the novice is magnetically drawn to it. He fights this presence and is saved from the maelstrom by the warm, red tracery of light shining through a stained-glass window portrait of St. Francis Xavier, the Spanish priest who had helped Ignatius establish the Jesuit order. This light mingles with and overpowers the candle glow, and the exposed Eucharist in the monstrance seems "very mystical and sweet." The flame of the altar candle goes out, the words of absolution are intoned, and the novice goes forward to take his vows. It is not at all sure that the novice's triumph is a permanent one, for Fitzgerald's ambivalence in this story is too apparent for us to believe in the happy ending. Xavier saves the novice this time, but sound religious vocations are not built upon such hairbreadth escapes from temptation. His worldly visions, and especially the specter of the masked destroyer, are likely to return to haunt the novice again, and a few years later, burnished by recurrent moments in his private hell, he might very well be the one to tempt a younger man. Just like Fitzgerald's other fictional brothers, the novice will be unable to resist the lure of the City of Man and its most dangerous attraction, Woman.

Five years later, when Fitzgerald wrote "Benediction," which owes its setting, theme, and tone to "The Ordeal," he was not more sure of his attitudes toward his religion. But one thing is certain: "Benediction" manifestly represents the religious sensibility which never left him, even after he publicly denounced the Church. The physical setting is the same as that of "The Ordeal," but the seminary in "Benediction" [91] is an intellectually attractive place, for the students carry volumes of Aquinas, Henry James, Cardinal Mercier, and Kant. The protagonist is not a novice, but a green-eyed nineteen-year-old girl visiting her older brother, who is just completing his eighteen-year preparation for ordination. Lois has come to this holy sanctuary after having agreed to an affair; and although she had anticipated a rather solemn visit, she finds herself "absurdly happy" in the company of her brother Keith and his friends, who are content and assured in their childlike faith.

Lois and Keith discuss their ineffectual mother (there is no father in the background), Keith's mystical experience, which had decided him on the priesthood after a wild adolescence, and his subsequent growth into the tolerance, humility, and impersonality of the priestly life. Lois argues for the desirability of worldliness, but Keith's hard and strong sweetness disarms her. The benediction scene from "The Ordeal" is repeated, but this time the green-eyed doubter is at the center of the crisis. Lois faints after the candle flame is extinguished by the goodness streaming through the saint in the window, and she feels that her naked soul has been held up to someone's scrutiny and ridicule. Unlike the novice who had been momentarily strengthened for his vows by this spiritual experience, Lois now militantly asserts to her brother the inconvenience of being a Catholic, the narrowness and irrelevance of Catholicism in her life. Keith answers with an admonition Father Fay had given Fitzgerald: "There's that gift of faith that we have, you and I, that carry us past the hard spots" (154). As Keith kneels for hours in prayer and meditation, Lois leaves first to cancel and then let stand her assignation with her lover. The worldly, human part of her wins out over her "broken and chastened" soul that had been touched in the chapel. In this sister and brother Fitzgerald objectified the Augustinian antithesis within himself of, on one hand, worldliness, sensuality, and weakness and, on the other, faith, asceticism, and devotion to an ideal. All his life this tension would burden him, yet, after all, it helped to produce his art. It is consistent with his sexual attitudes, and it is in the Augustinian tradition that he identified the experiencing but morally weak part of himself as female and the morally strong and transcendent part as male.

In both "The Ordeal" and "Benediction" Fitzgerald's unusual use of light imagery anticipates its importance in "Absolution" and *The Great Gatsby*. In each story, light, which is symbolic of grace, blessed knowledge or, in short, the essence of all that is good, represents the essence of evil. In these early stories, then, we find the Augustinian antitheses of sacred and secular, spirit and flesh, the City of God and the City of Man, candle and carnival light which would become a central element of the later stories and novels. Perhaps Fitzgerald's unorthodox use of symbolism in these stories as well as his growing apostasy caused some uneasiness in him which he projected to Catholic commentators, for he claimed that in the critical reception of "Benediction" and "Absolution" there was much hostility. In fact, they received favorable reaction from Catholic publications. Fitzgerald complained to a friend that "the story 'Benediction' that received the imprimatur of the most intelligent priest I know [Father Joseph Barron] has come in for the most terrible lashing from the American Catholic intelligentsia," and he concluded that "an American [Catholic writer] had better have his works either pious tracts for nuns or else disassociate them from the Church as a living issue." [92] But his assessment of Catholic opinion is contravened by the praise of *Catholic World* for all of the stories in *Flappers and Philosophers,* his 1920 volume of short stories which includes "Benediction." The critic must have seen that the emotional balance in the story is tipped in favor of Keith and the spiritual life and against Lois and her rejection of the palpable values of the pious Catholic life at the monastery and the meaning of the epiphany in the chapel.

In 1920, when "Benediction" was written, Father Fay was dead, Zelda Sayre had come into Fitzgerald's life and had replaced all other objects of his adoration, and he had abandoned all thoughts of the priesthood. He must have known that his temperament and ambitions could not be expressed in the priestly life. No thunderbolt from heaven had come to deny this, and in his spiritual immaturity he apparently considered this sort of miraculous sign the essence of the religious experience. After his marriage, Fitzgerald turned his back on Catholicism; the absolutism of his Catholic training was strong in him, and it worked in him to defeat its own purpose. Fitzgerald always respected genuine faith, however, and his "holy sonnet," "The Pope at Confession," written while he was at Princeton and still an observing Catholic, clearly points up his admiration for true piety.

The gorgeous Vatican was steeped in night,
The organs trembled to my heart no more,
But with the blend of colors in my sight
I loitered through a sombre corridor
And suddenly I heard behind a screen
The faintest whisper, as from one in prayer,
I glanced around, then passed, for I had seen
A hushed and lonely room . . . and two were there—
A ragged friar, half in a dream's embrace
Leaned sideways, soul intent, as if to seize
The last gray ice of sin that ached to melt
And faltered from the lips of him who knelt—
A little bent old man upon his knees
With pain and sorrow in his holy face.[93]

The image of the infallible pope, the vicar of Christ and king of Christ's earthly kingdom, is given another dimension here. He is humanly capable of sin and bears pain and sorrow in humility as he submits himself to be shriven by a lowly friar.

Apparently Father Fay's campaign to keep alive the latent Catholicism in Fitzgerald had been at least partially successful. The priest visited Fitzgerald at Princeton and took him and some other Newman graduates to dinner, but for Fitzgerald he reserved the privilege of weekends at his mother's house in Deal and visits to the Chanlers and other wealthy New York homes. Fay also introduced Fitzgerald to Father William Hemmick, an urbane and literary man. Fay had made Fitzgerald see the Church as a "dazzling, golden thing," a glamorous international church that had nothing to do with the provincial experience of the typical American Catholic; and William Hemmick, with his cassocks tailored in Paris, silver-buckled pumps, and urbane air, was an incarnation of this brand of Catholicism. Fitzgerald knew him at Newman, and later during his army service corresponded with him. However, knowledge of the breadth and character of this relationship is lost to us, for Shane Leslie reported in 1958 that Hemmick had destroyed Fitzgerald's letters.[94] It is regrettable that apparently Hemmick's profound disappointment at Fitzgerald's

failure to become the American Robert Hugh Benson, as he and
Fay and Leslie had urged, outweighed his sense of responsibility to
the world of letters.[95]

William Hemmick was born in Pittsburgh in 1886. His father,
Roland Hemmick, was an officer of the United States Foreign
Service, which accounts for his son's European education and
lifelong preference for things Continental. The high point of the
senior Hemmick's career was service as consul general in Switzer-
land. Father Hemmick received his undergraduate education at
the Jesuit College in Feldkirch, Austria, and he studied at Catholic
University in Washington where he met Father Fay, who was
teaching sacred liturgy and ecclesiastical Greek. Hemmick spent
only a few years in America before his permanent expatriation
began with his service as an army chaplain in France during World
War I. He remained in Paris for the next decade, and there he was
visited by prominent American Catholic travelers and often by
Shane Leslie, who had returned to England.

Hemmick was made a monsignor and was called to Rome in
1932, and after a time he became the first American priest to be
named a canon of St. Peter's Basilica. There he served as
ecclesiastical attaché to the embassy of the Sovereign Order of
Malta, a post that gave him diplomatic status and kept him in
touch with ambassadors and their aides. He continued to receive
visitors in Rome as he had in Paris until his residence became an
obligatory stop for many American tourists. At the time of his
death in September 1971, Monsignor Hemmick had been living
for many years in the Doria Palace located in the center of Rome,
a home which was owned by a family of old Roman nobility.
Hemmick was known for his fluency in several languages, his great
store of Vatican anecdotes, and the fact that the Swedish princess
who later became Queen Astrid of Belgium was among his many
converts.[96] Hemmick was a society priest, and the part of
Fitzgerald impressed by the appearances of wealth was drawn to
this anachronistic practitioner of the old church art of ministering
to aristocracy.

Another of the "fireside group" at the Newman School, an
informal meeting of selected "old boys" including Fay and
Hemmick, was Shane Leslie, a minor English novelist who taught

briefly at Newman after Fay became its headmaster in 1913. Leslie, the first professional writer to advise Fitzgerald, was the son of an Anglo-Irish baronet, a cousin of Winston Churchill, and a chamberlain to the pope, a singular honor for a layman. Leslie was educated at Eton and Cambridge; he knew Tolstoy and Rupert Brooke; and he was altogether the most romantic figure Fitzgerald had ever known. In obvious hyperbole Leslie said that to have seen Fitzgerald and Fay together "was to have realized . . . an Alexander tutored by an Aristotle," [97] for Fay "had trained and civilized Fitzgerald, a boy from the wilds of Minnesota." [98] Leslie was also a convert to Catholicism, and with Fay he tried to attract Fitzgerald to the excitement they saw in the Church. When he began to show serious literary ambition, they did everything they could to make him the American counterpart of Robert Hugh Benson, the English Catholic novelist-priest and son of the Archbishop of Canterbury.

Father Fay told Leslie that Fitzgerald thought it "clever and literary" to rebel against his upbringing and the Church and that they must attempt to save him from apostasy. With Father Hemmick they tried to guide his reading to Benson and the novels of Compton MacKenzie, also a Catholic convert. For a time, Fitzgerald assumed the persona of Michael Fane, a convert and the hero of *Youth's Encounter* and *Sinister Street*, two novels which profoundly influenced *This Side of Paradise*. Fay and Leslie also talked in his presence about accomplished men in the Church like Augustine and Newman, and they took him to a reception for the duc de Richelieu where he happily consumed great quantities of champagne and fraternized with prominent Catholics. But the combined force of this trio, Fay, Leslie, and Hemmick, was not enough to capture Fitzgerald once and for all. Away from the direct influence of a Catholic community, in the exuberant and secular atmosphere at Princeton, Fitzgerald had been straying from the Church. He would struggle for a time to attend mass and observe fast and abstinence regulations, and he would talk of becoming a priest, but then he would slip and feel guilty. After a conversation with Fitzgerald about his religion, a young professor told another student that he felt that Fitzgerald was going through some sort of spiritual crisis.[99]

In the summer of 1917, Fay proposed a project that captured Fitzgerald's imagination and brought him more nearly back to the faith than anything else the priest had tried. Father Fay was interested in the state of the Russian Church, for the Kerensky revolution had estranged the Orthodox Church from its Tsarist associations, and Fay saw himself as a key figure in the restoration of Catholic unity. Cardinal Gibbons agreed to cooperate in Fay's secret mission to Russia under the guise of a Red Cross project, and Fay wanted Fitzgerald to go along with the rank of a Red Cross lieutenant. Fitzgerald spent a month at the home of John Bishop in West Virginia waiting for the adventure to materialize, and he returned to strict religious observance and talked a great deal of becoming a priest until Bishop's mother feared that her son would be converted through Fitzgerald's zeal. But conditions in Russia were extremely unsettled, and Gibbons withdrew his approval, so Fay immediately planned to involve Fitzgerald in another secret mission, this time to Rome.

Fay sailed to Europe as a deputy commissioner of the American Red Cross with the rank of major in the United States Army, and he sent reports of his Vatican conferences to Cardinal Gibbons in the British diplomatic pouch. The Pope wanted Gibbons's help in influencing President Wilson to strike from the secret Treaty of London (April 26, 1915) a clause excluding the Vatican from the Versailles Peace Conference. In that treaty France, Great Britian, and Russia agreed to support Italy's opposition to Vatican representation in the peace negotiations in exchange for Italy's entering the war on the side of the Allies.[100] Fay had to tell the Pope that Wilson would not cooperate, but the pontiff was disarmed by Fay's candor and charm, and he made him a monsignor.[101] When he returned to America, Monsignor Fay became Pope Benedict XV's champion. He gave a series of lectures on Benedict's involvement in the European conflict at Carnegie Hall in New York and in Boston, Philadelphia, and Baltimore.[102] He also wrote an article for *The Chronicle,* the Baltimore diocesan newspaper, to counteract propaganda against the Vatican's supposed pro-German sentiments. Fay pointed out that the Pope was the only nonbelligerent who had protested the rape of Belgium, the subsequent bombing of unarmed towns, unrestricted submarine warfare, and the deportation of Belgians.[103]

It had not been possible for Fitzgerald to go to Rome, and he had to be content with letters from Fay in which he attempted to deal with Fitzgerald's spiritual turmoil and to keep him close. Fay wrote: "Now as to your moral reflections. . . . The fear of God is your greatest frustration as it is mine, nor could you rid yourself of it if you would—it will all ways [sic] be there. [We are both] religious but not conventionally pious"; [104] and "You make a great mistake is that you think you can be romantic without religion. None of us can. . . . I discover that if I did not have a good hold on the mystical side of religion the romance would have died down considerably." [105] But with Father Fay away and his chance for a diplomatic adventure lost, Fitzgerald abandoned his short-lived piety.

Not all of Fitzgerald's turmoil during his years at Princeton was spiritual, for when he was nineteen and a sophomore, he fell in love with Ginevra King, the daughter of a wealthy Chicago industrialist whom he had met in St. Paul where during the Christmas holiday she was visiting a mutual friend. They spent only a little time together, but after she returned to Westover and he to Princeton, they exchanged long letters (Fitzgerald kept all of hers and had them typed and bound years later), and he visited her at her school. He thought he had found his Golden Girl. Her wealth and her need for constant attention from many men, however, sent him periodically into despair. "Poor boys shouldn't think of marrying rich girls" (170), he wrote in his Ledger, and a year later Fitzgerald gave up the pursuit of Ginevra when he saw that it was hopeless. But she had become an indelible part of his concept of Woman, and until he met Zelda Sayre, she was the model in his fiction of the vampiric destroyer.

At this point in his life Fitzgerald's sexual ambivalence was evident. The essential doubleness expressed in his statement, " . . . the test of a first-rate intelligence is the ability to hold two opposed ideas in the mind at the same time, and still retain the ability to function," [106] is reflected in his attitude toward sex. A part of him disapproved of a girl like Ginevra, a "speed," "a sensation and a scandal; [who] had driven mature men to a state of disequilibrium; [107] yet this is the kind of woman he had to have for himself and whom he made the heroine of his stories and of the Jazz Age. At an age when most young men, especially those who are handsome and are interested in and sought after by women, are at their sexual peak and feel sexual urges most strongly, Fitzgerald was actually puritanical. A young woman whom he met in the summer of 1917, when he was staying with the Bishops, reports that

> He was always trying to see how far he could go in arousing your feelings, but it was always with words. . . . The Southern boys I knew . . . at least understood what it was all about, and were more aggressive and emotionally satisfying. . . . I'm afraid, Scott just wasn't a very lively male animal. . . . His mouth was his most revealing feature. . . . All his Midwestern puritanism was there. He had never lived in that magnetic world of the senses.[108]

Yet opposed to this puritanism in Fitzgerald there was an aberrant and extreme vulgarity which showed up years later. When he was sober he was prudish and would not tolerate rough language or suggestiveness, but when he had been drinking and his inhibitions were relaxed he tried to shock others with his personal sexual revelations, intrusive questions about his friends' sexual practices, and objectionable language. He said he loathed pornography, and, referring to a ribald memoir, told a woman friend, "It's disgusting. It's the kind of filth your sex is often subjected to, the kind of lavatory conversation men indulge in . . . you don't know how disgusting men can be!" [109] Yet some of his letters to Hemingway and Edmund Wilson contain extremely coarse passages and scurrilous references to women and homosexuals. He hated "filth," yet among his papers is a brochure for *The Scented Garden,* a volume euphemistically advertised as one "Sold only by subscription to physicians, lawyers and adult students of sexual anthropology." [110]

Fitzgerald was sharply critical of other Princetonians' casual sexual encounters, and he had the reputation of a person of

seriousness, even prudishness, about sex. He once remarked after
seeing a friend pursuing a girl on Nassau Street, "That's one thing
Fitzgerald has never done!" [111] In his junior year he was forced to
leave school for a time because of illness, and when he returned, he
learned that he had lost the presidency of the Triangle Club. It
seemed to him that he had lost everything of value, and in a
desperate evening, for the first time he "hunted down the spectre of
womanhood that, for a little while, makes everything else seem
unimportant." [112] Thus as a student he lost his virginity with a
Princeton prostitute. That he went to a woman for comfort was
predictable and usual, but that he should refer to her as a
"spectre" is strange. Fitzgerald's fastidiousness and orthodox sense
of morality were noted by Ernest Boyd in his 1924 biographical
sketch:

> There are still venial and mortal sins in his calendar, and . . .
> his Catholic heaven is not so far away that he can be misled
> into mistaking the shoddy dreams of a radical millennium as a
> substitute for Paradise. . . . His Confessions, if he ever writes
> any, will make the reader envy his transgressions, for they will
> be permeated by the conviction of sin, which is much happier
> than the conviction that the way to Utopia is paved with
> adultery.[113]

Boyd astutely used the language of Catholicism in his account
of Fitzgerald's moral posture, but it was perhaps too early in
Fitzgerald's career for Boyd to note that he had already started to
write his confessions, which were, indeed, permeated by the
conviction of sin.

In his years at Princeton, through his failures as a student and
campus Big Man, his religious crises, and his problems with
Ginevra King and his sexual ambivalence, Fitzgerald conclusively
had become a writer. He had learned little from the academicians,
for he had rejected the traditional education they offered and
instead chose the tutelage of John Peale Bishop and Edmund
Wilson. In the fall of 1917, Fitzgerald returned to Princeton to wait
out the arrival of his army commission, knowing that it was time

for him to move on. He had caught the infectious excitement of the war, and he was eager to meet his gloriously heroic end on the battlefield. In November, Fitzgerald was commissioned an army second lieutenant and left behind the things of his boyhood for what he hoped would be his final adventure.

2.

Early Success: 1917-1920

A story published in the June 1917 issue of the *Nassau Literary Magazine* is a good index of Fitzgerald's condition as he faced the prospect of war; it also reflects his bewilderment at the "new morality" he saw evolving around him. His New England conscience developed in Minnesota, the moralism that had been engendered in him by his early Catholic training, and his essential romanticism were outraged by the sexual permissiveness of his contemporaries. His impulse to preach at people rather than to entertain them clearly is evident in the story "Sentiment and the Use of Rouge." [1] Clay Syneforth, a young English lieutenant, has returned to London after two years in the war, and he is appalled by the profusion of paint worn by young women, which seems to him a signpost of the breakdown of values and social distinctions which have occurred in his absence. He is both fascinated and repelled by the hedonism he sees around him, and he tries to hold fast to the morality of his father's generation, to which he had always subscribed.

Clay returns to the war and a death scene played out with an Irish soldier who observes that "blood on an Englishman always calls rouge . . . to mind. It's a game with him. The Irish take death damn serious" (155). Not burdened with abstractions, and especially the notion that God is an Englishman, O'Flaherty dies well, saying the Hail Mary. Clay envies the Irishman's simplicity and the comfort his religion has given him, and as his own death approaches, he tries to find O'Flaherty's God. But he is too inhibited by the stiff-upper-lip code of his class to be in touch with his own elemental spiritual needs. His idea of religion has been a tangible, practical one, and he had thought of God, when he did think of God, as an M.P. at large or as residing somewhere in the arched solemnity of Westminster Abbey. He dies, true to English form as O'Flaherty described it, looking for the Referee to bring order out of the "damned muddle" of the war and the social and moral chaos it has caused. The shibboleth "for God and country" had equipped him to face the perils of a changing order with only a stuffy priggishness and a sterile sort of spirituality. Fitzgerald confided to friends that he expected to die in battle and that he, like O'Flaherty, "May get killed for me flag, but I'm goin to die for meself" (157).

Before Fitzgerald left Princeton to begin his army career, he wrote to his mother about two old issues; money, which had made their relationship uneasy for years; and religion, which with his movement toward apostasy was becoming a sore point between them.

My uniforms are going to cost quite a bit so if you haven't sent me what you have of *my own money* please do so. . . . If you want to pray for my soul and not that I won't get killed—the last doesn't seem to matter particularly and if you are a good Catholic the first ought to.[2]

The irony in this letter probably had more to do with Fitzgerald's troubled feelings for his mother than with anti-Catholic sentiment, for in 1930, in explaining his fearlessness at going to war, he wrote, "I was . . . then a Roman Catholic, which meant heaven." [3] The war was a social event that he did not want to miss, but Fort Leavenworth in Kansas, where he was sent for basic training, was like a prison after Princeton. There he spent every free moment in work on "The Romantic Egoist," the novel he had begun a few months earlier at Princeton at Monsignor Fay's suggestion. Within five months the manuscript was on its way to Shane Leslie for his criticism and his help in finding a publisher. Leslie gave the manuscript to Scribner's and asked them to hold it because he wanted its author to go off to war thinking he had written a publishable novel. Fitzgerald valued Leslie's literary opinions, and he found Leslie's analysis of Ireland's dilemma in the contemporary European situation helpful in his own search for his Irish identity. In his review of *The Celt and the World* for the May 1917 issue of the *Nassau Literary Magazine*, Fitzgerald called the book "a bible of Irish patriotism." It made him acutely aware of Ireland's situation, and it gave him "an intense desire to see Ireland free at last to work out her own destiny under Home Rule ... directly under the eyes of God." [4]

While the "The Romantic Egoist" manuscript was in Leslie's hands, Monsignor Fay was in Rome, for the priest had asked his friend to act as Fitzgerald's literary mentor in his absence. As Leslie puts it, "I can claim to have been his [Fitzgerald's] inventor and originator in America in 1917-1918. His beloved master and pastor, Monsignor Cyril Fay, brought him to me as one in some need of advice and encouragement." [5] Years later Leslie based his claim to a major share of the credit for the success of *This Side of Paradise* on the fact that he "sat down and in ten days improved it [the "The Romantic Egoist" manuscript] grammatically and cut up the paragraphs." [6] Fitzgerald did carry over some materials from the earlier manuscript to *This Side of Paradise,* but they are not in any sense the same book. This claim is as spurious as Leslie's assertion that "Fitz married on the resounding success of the novel I had carefully corrected. ... They [Fitzgerald and his wife] took the trouble to travel to Europe to thank me for my part in their triumph." [7] Leslie later became a dubious ally, [8] but, whatever his motives, he was a help to the young writer whose first novel had been rejected.

Scribner's returned "The Romantic Egoist" to Fitzgerald in October 1918, and Leslie then encouraged him to revise it carefully and to "*see* that it will be possible for Roman Catholic papers ... to say a word for the book." [9] He was still hoping that Fitzgerald would follow the line of Robert Hugh Benson, and he apparently had received some encouragement from Fitzgerald, for he recorded in his diary that Scott was thinking of "taking the priesthood." [10]

During this time Monsignor Fay wrote concerned letters to his absent son who was in spiritual difficulty. We can only infer what Fitzgerald must have written to the priest to have elicited this response: "As to women it is not convention that holds you back as you think but an instinct that if you once begin—you will run amuck." [11] However, no measure of priestly commiseration or admonition could stay the changes wrought in Fitzgerald's life by a girl barely eighteen when they met.

His novel completed, Fitzgerald had time to spare, and he joined the social life open to army officers in Montgomery. Before he met and was captivated by Zelda Sayre, Fitzgerald spent much time with a Catholic girl in Montgomery. In spite of his spiritual turmoil, he apparently was still a practicing Catholic, for one afternoon as they were walking in town, they passed a Catholic church, and Fitzgerald decided to go to confession. After he was finished, he persuaded the girl that she, too, should confess. When she stopped after recounting several minor sins, the priest urged her to continue. He insisted that she had more to tell him since he had already heard her "young man's" confession. Fitzgerald was not amused by this breach of sacramental confidence, and it only intensified his turmoil.[12]

Each Saturday night Fitzgerald went to the country club dance, and there on a July evening he met Zelda. From then on he spent every bit of free time with her. The Sayres had some reservations about Fitzgerald—his not having graduated from Princeton, his Yankee background, and his religion were things to which they objected—but they were not able to influence Zelda's choice of companions. He was handsome and polite, and they were inclined to be grateful to anyone who could stabilize their daughter's madcap behavior. Fitzgerald read to her what he was writing and found her comments and suggestions valuable. He learned then that beneath her spectacular exterior there was a keen intelligence and perceptiveness, and he would draw upon this reservoir of support all their life together. They shared a vitality and an appetite for fun, and in the first months of their courtship they achieved an intimacy they would never quite be able to duplicate.

Scott proposed often, and Zelda, genuinely in love and at last excited by his promises of fame and excitement as the wife of a celebrated writer, agreed to marry him. It is not clear whether or not they were lovers during this time, but the evidence seems to support the opinion that they were. Zelda apparently never mentioned it, but years later, in a narrative about their marriage which he was asked to write by her therapist, Fitzgerald said that she had been his mistress for a year before their marriage, and he complained about her sexual recklessness. Their physical separation for much of that time would have made a relationship which the word "mistress" implies impossible, but Fitzgerald's obsessive questions to friends about their premarital relations indicate that he was deeply troubled by the subject. His intense guilt, his deep sense of commitment to Zelda, and his acute despair after she broke their engagement point to the fact that their relationship was more serious than any other he had known. With his old Catholic habit of mind, Fitzgerald considered sex a very serious matter, and he, like Gatsby with Daisy, felt that, in the consummation of their affair, he had married Zelda. The affair of Gatsby and Daisy, which he described as almost a sacramental gesture, and the guilt-ridden affair of Anthony Patch and Dorothy Raycroft in *The Beautiful and Damned* are ways in which Fitzgerald dealt in his fiction with his own ambivalent feelings.

Fitzgerald was sent in November to Long Island to await embarkation orders, but the war ended before his division could leave. This disappointment and his football failures were wounds he would scratch at and reopen all his life. When he returned to Camp Sheridan he was reunited with Zelda, and they were together on an evening when Fitzgerald felt a premonition of something terribly wrong. The next morning he received a telegram from the headmaster of the Newman School informing him that Monsignor Fay had died of influenza. Fay had been ill for days, but he refused to rest and kept his promise to preach for Cardinal Gibbons at the cathedral in Baltimore and the next day at a retreat in New York.[13] Fitzgerald expressed his profound grief in a letter to the headmaster in which he said that this news was the greatest shock of his life. He had looked to Fay, he said, before anyone else; he felt like "the dregs of a cup," for the best was over.

Fitzgerald and Leslie exchanged a flurry of letters at this time, some of which Fitzgerald used in his description of Monsignor Darcy's funeral in *This Side of Paradise*. Leslie used this sad time and Fitzgerald's emotion to try to keep him near with the words: "There is nothing left except the Church and for that reason we must keep our lamps alive. ... Take heart. ... Read widely and well until Father Hemmick returns." Leslie suggested that Fitzgerald would be happier if he were anchored to the priesthood, and he reminded Fitzgerald that Fay had always wanted him to be a priest. Leslie cautioned him not to "rush into Bohemia—Rome is the only permanent country the only patria to which we can all belong." [14] Monsignor Fay had, in fact, intended to designate Leslie as Fitzgerald's spiritual father in his will, and Leslie appealed to Fitzgerald to transfer his trust and affection to him. Fitzgerald answered that his world had been shattered by the death of Fay and that he was "nearly sure" that he would become a priest. Leslie observed years later that had Monsignor Fay lived, Fitzgerald would have tried valiantly to remain a Catholic. But the beloved priest, his second father, was dead, and Zelda Sayre took his place in Fitzgerald's life.

Some have taken the 1917 Ledger entry, "A year of enormous importance. Work, and Zelda. Last year as a Catholic" (172), to be the literal truth.[15] There are several problems with such literalism. We have seen that in the composition of the Ledger, Fitzgerald's memory was not totally reliable. In this case, his chronology is wrong, for he did not meet Zelda until July, 1918. Therefore, this entry reflects the events of 1918, the year in which he wrote "The Romantic Egoist" and met his future wife. The phrase, "Last year as a Catholic," was in all probability a reflection of the spiritual turmoil we have seen him experiencing at this time rather than an absolute rejection of his religion. That Fitzgerald should link Zelda and what for the time he felt was the end of his Catholicism is understandable and congruent with things he said elsewhere. In a letter to a friend he said, "I love her and that's the beginning and end of everything. You're still a Catholic but Zelda's the only God I have left now." [16] Fitzgerald apparently rejected his essentially romantic and tenuous thoughts of the priesthood when he met Zelda, but his disavowal of Catholicism at this point in his life is to be discounted for several reasons. If in his statement, "Last year as a Catholic," he meant separation from the Church, it is not true, for he was married by a priest in 1920, and his daughter was baptized and sponsored by his good friend Father Joseph Barron a year later. If he meant that it would be possible for him to escape the Catholic influences of his past, then his change of mind can be seen in a 1928 interview in which he stated that among the chief early influences in his life was the Roman Catholic Church.[17]

Fitzgerald spent six unsuccessful months in New York, where he supported himself with a job in an advertising agency and attempted to make his way as a writer. He was able to sell just one story; already published in the *Nassau Literary Magazine* at Princeton, it appeared in Mencken's *Smart Set*. Discouraged by his failure to inaugurate the great literary career he had promised Zelda and by their broken engagement, in July, Fitzgerald left New York and returned to St. Paul, where, in an ascetic three months, he reworked the material of "The Romantic Egoist" to produce *This Side of Paradise*. Scribner's enthusiastically accepted it in September, and Fitzgerald naively asked for immediate publication because he had so many things depending upon success, "including of course a girl." Fitzgerald's relationship with his family during this summer in St. Paul was strained. They supplied him with a room and bare sustenance while he was absorbed in an enterprise of which they, with the exception of his father, disapproved, and he had to depend upon friends for cigarettes and other small luxuries.

There was parental pressure in another area, too, for Fitzgerald noted in his Ledger that his mother was buying him religious books, for she, like Shane Leslie, saw that his days as a practicing Catholic were numbered.[18] Mrs. Fitzgerald blamed her son's apostasy on the influences of the Protestant college he had attended and the godless writers he had read there. (Of course, Monsignor Fay had introduced him to the decadent fin de siècle writers as well as to Benson.) Fitzgerald's defection from Catholicism was inevitable, and no amount of parental concern and prompting could have prevented it, but Mrs. Fitzgerald would periodically attempt to bring her son back to the fold. Shane Leslie was using another tactic to accomplish the same end. He suggested that Fitzgerald write an article for the *Dublin Review* about St.

Paul's Archbishop John Ireland. Since Fitzgerald would have had to spend much time in the diocesan archives and in conversation with clergy, Leslie hoped that this activity and contact would have a salutary effect upon his protégé. There is no evidence that Fitzgerald ever gave any consideration to this project. Another friend, Edmund Wilson, was pulling at Fitzgerald from another direction. He asked Fitzgerald to contribute to a volume of war stories he was compiling, and he told Fitzgerald to clear his mind of cant, to "forget for a moment the phosphorescences of the decaying Church of Rome!" [19] Fitzgerald did not send a story, but in a letter to Wilson he assessed the state of his Catholicism: "I am ashamed to say that my Catholicism is scarcely more than a memory—no that's wrong, it's more than that; at any rate I go not to church nor mumble stray nothings over crystalline beads." [20] Mrs. Fitzgerald's campaign to bring her son back to the Church was relentless; Fitzgerald's Ledger contains an entry for October 1919: "Mother's suggestion of dots [ellipsis] in purifying Head and Shoulders" (174). Fitzgerald's sale of this story, which began his long and lucrative association with the *Saturday Evening Post,* reinforced his sense of having fulfilled his promises to Zelda. A few weeks later he returned to Montgomery to urge her to resume their engagement, and she agreed to marry him even before the great fame and success that followed the publication of his novel could have been evident to her. The picture of Zelda demanding success and wealth from Fitzgerald, which he largely created and perpetuated, is a distorted one. It was he who had been taught that money is a symbol of beatitude, and this he taught his young wife, whose own meager education could not supply her with a better alternative.

On March 20, 1920, Judge and Mrs. Sayre announced the engagement, and, on March 26, *This Side of Paradise* was published. They decided to be married eight days later in New York. Fitzgerald insisted on a Catholic ceremony, and the Sayres were probably relieved to be spared the embarrassment this would have caused in Montgomery. Zelda's family had at first objected to Fitzgerald's religion, which was anathema in this citadel of the Protestant Confederacy, but when they saw that Zelda was determined to have him, they were gracious about it. Mrs. Sayre told Fitzgerald, "A good Catholic is as good as any other man and that is good enough. It will take more than the Pope to make Zelda good; you will have to call on God Almighty direct." [21] Fitzgerald's parents did not meet Zelda until the couple arrived in St. Paul shortly before the birth of their daughter in 1921. At the time of the marriage, all the Fitzgeralds knew about Zelda was that she was a southern Protestant girl; the former must have pleased Fitzgerald's father, but the latter could only have caused his mother consternation. Although Zelda had been baptized at the Episcopal Church of the Holy Comforter in Montgomery when she was ten and as a child had regularly attended Sunday school, she was not confirmed, nor was she a churchgoer,[22] the least Mrs. Fitzgerald would have settled for.

Fitzgerald made the arrangements for the wedding even before Zelda arrived in New York. He wanted it done quickly and with little ceremony, and perhaps did not encourage their parents to attend. The ceremony took place on the morning of April 3, 1920, in the rectory of St. Patrick's Cathedral. The officiating priest was the Reverend W. B. Martin, a staff priest who was unknown to them.[23] The only people present were Zelda's two sisters, Marjorie and Rosalind; Rosalind's husband Newman Smith, who was a witness; and Ludlow Fowler, a Princeton classmate of Fitzgerald's, who was the best man. After the service, Father Martin said to them, "You be a good Episcopalian, Zelda, and, Scott, you be a good Catholic, and you'll get along fine." [24]

The Fitzgerald marriage, which was correct canonically if not liturgically, as Fitzgerald told Shane Leslie, had begun on an austere note. But this mood was short-lived, for within a few days the management of their hotel asked them to leave because of the disturbances they caused. A few weeks later, Fitzgerald was suspended from his Princeton club after a riotous weekend during which he introduced Zelda as his mistress. The Jazz Age had begun.

This Side of Paradise

Fitzgerald's first novel was a great success. In its first year it led the Scribner list with sales of almost 50,000 copies, and its author was both vilified and hailed for his revelations of the mores of the young. The book brought the Fitzgeralds instant fame and celebrity, and its momentum made them the darlings of the Jazz Age. *This Side of Paradise*, in which Fitzgerald imitated the models of Robert Hugh Benson, Compton MacKenzie, Wells, Tarkington, and others, is written in an episodic and discursive style the vogue of which is long past. Its central character, Amory Blaine, calls this sort of novel a "quest book," and it is surely more a *Bildungsroman* than a *Künstlerroman*, for Amory, merely a dilettante writer at Princeton, is never believable as an artist. If it were not for the obvious parallels between Fitzgerald and Amory, it would probably not occur to the reader that Amory will eventually make his way as a writer. Fitzgerald was more concerned with Amory's social nature than his psychological or emotional life; consequently *This Side of Paradise*, Fitzgerald's most sustained overtly Catholic piece of fiction, is more a sociological than a literary event, and it is interesting mainly for what it reveals of Fitzgerald's artistic development rather than for its dubious literary value.

The antecedent of *This Side of Paradise* is "The Romantic Egoist," the first version of which has not survived. However, five chapters of the first-person second version are among the Fitzgerald Papers, and they are the only evidence we have of the nature of the manuscript that had been rejected twice by Scribner's. In it Fitzgerald devoted four chapters to his early boyhood and prep-school experiences which he would use later in the Basil stories. The manuscript is interesting for its biographical implications for this period, and especially for a view of Fitzgerald's evolving image of himself in relation to his family and his social and religious background. Stephen Palms, the hero of "The Romantic Egoist," [25] shares Amory Blaine's and Fitzgerald's conviction that anything worthwhile he has in the way of brains and energy comes from his mother's Irish family. His dubious forebear on his father's side is not Francis Scott Key, but Benedict Arnold, and from his father he had acquired an "extended and showy, if very superficial knowledge of the Civil War (with an intense Southern bias)" (4). Stephen's father is not a prominent character, he dies on page six, but he is a relatively more fully drawn character than Stephen Blaine, Amory's father. Material which derives from the "Death of My Father" manuscript, which is duplicated in the reminiscences of Dick Diver about his boyhood, is an important part of the ambivalent portrait of Stephen's father. There had been real affection between the elder Palms and his son, but he had given Stephen a doubtful patrimony. Apparently the accommodation of his image of his father which Fitzgerald had expressed in "Shadow Laurels" had broken down, and he had not yet reached the equanimity of Dick Diver's view.

Stephen, more truly than Amory Blaine a picture of the young Fitzgerald, describes his lie during confession, his confessing this sin two years later, and his resignation from the YMCA after he learned that Catholics could not hold office. Stephen had been reading Cobbett's *History of the Protestant Reformation,* one of the volumes in Fitzgerald's library, "and was crammed full of bigotry" (23). He discusses sex with a girl in Minneapolis [Basil's and Fitzgerald's St. Paul], where he is sequestered like Amory for a few years, and he shares Amory's extreme puritanical response in sexual matters. In describing the denouement of their relationship, Stephen says that only the good luck of his having been sent off to summer camp saved them from a catastrophe. The first two chapters of "The Romantic Egoist" take Stephen through his entry into the Markle School, a name altered from the Newman School in the manuscript, and the other two chapters are early versions of the Eleanor and Devil episodes in *This Side of Paradise.*

One of the most interesting aspects of "The Romantic Egoist" is Stephen Palms's fantasy about his lineage.

> I was sure . . . that I was not the son of my parents. To bear this out I often acted the part of an amateur foundling and told the neighbors that I had been found one cold night on the doorstep with a piece of paper that I claimed Mother still had—on which was written one word "Stuart."(6)

Fitzgerald's Ledger contains two entries which echo this: "He . . . told enormous lies to older people about being really the owner of a real yatch [sic]" and "Suspicion that he is a changeling" [155]. This sort of statement and Stephen's fantasy are symptomatic of the phenomenon Freud called the "family romance," which is one of the several aspects of the oedipal conflict. The family romance grows out of a child's effort to emancipate himself from his parents and to surpass them. The family romance is different from this usual impulse, however, in that the child's shame of his parents gives rise to fantasies about his birth. The usual desire of the adolescent to desexualize the parents is logically worked out in his imagining that he is not the child of his parents at all. Part of the family romance pattern is the child's rejection of the real parents and the establishment of relationships with idealized adult replacements, or, in short, the search for a good father. Just as Stephen fantasizes about his lineage, as a child Fitzgerald told neighbors and friends that he was a foundling and a descendant of the Stuart kings. Subsequently a critical attitude toward and rejection of the parents became an essential experience, not only for him, but also for most of his characters.

The adult Fitzgerald documented the presence of his family romance in a 1936 *Esquire* article, "An Author's House." [26] In it Fitzgerald guides a narrator through a house which is a representation of the compartments of his experience—the components of the unconscious, memory, and the influences that have formed him. The cellar is his unconscious, and among its debris is everything he has forgotten, the complex dark mixture of his infancy and youth which made him a writer instead of a fireman or soldier. The agents are here, the things that led him to the sedentary days and sleepless nights and endless dissatisfaction of the writer's life. The writer points to a dark corner which contains the prenatal conditions of his existence. Three months before he was born his mother lost two children, and he thinks that then he started to be a writer. In answer to the narrator's question about a mound in a corner, the writer replies, "That is where I buried . . . my belief that I wasn't the son of my parents but a son of a king . . . who ruled the whole world" (184). Obviously it was not buried too deeply, for this fantasy is present in one way or another in each of Fitzgerald's novels and in many of the stories. The writer then traces his dependence upon alcohol back to the poor eating habits he had developed as a boy, probably a correlative of his inadequate patrimony. This is one of several instances of Fitzgerald's indictment of his family and his tendency to blame them for his deficiencies. His brains, energy, and ambition he, like

Amory, attributed to his mother's heritage, but his success, he felt, had been possible only through his following the oedipal impulse to replace or excel his father, a motive that Mollie Fitzgerald had encouraged in her son.

The troubled relationship of parent and child is central to the background of Amory Blaine and to his "quest book," *This Side of Paradise.*[27] Amory is introduced as the "Son of Beatrice" just as Fitzgerald had been known as "Mollie McQuillan's boy." There are some striking similarities and contrasts between the backgrounds of Beatrice O'Hara Blaine and Mollie McQuillan Fitzgerald, their Irishness being the first and most apparent characteristic. Both have wealthy fathers, but the O'Hara far exceeds the McQuillan fortune. Mollie McQuillan had traveled to Europe several times, but Beatrice passed her youth "in renaissance glory" in England, Vienna, and at the Sacred Heart Convent in Rome. Here she was known by cardinals and royalty, grand improvements on the Irish Catholic hierarchy and society figures of Mollie McQuillan's world in St. Paul. Beatrice is a Catholic, but she is urbanely and insouciantly religious while Mollie was conservatively and sincerely devout. Beatrice had discovered "that priests were infinitely more attentive when she was in the process of losing or regaining her faith in Mother Church, [so] she maintained an enchantingly wavering attitude . . . [for] next to doctors, priests were her favorite sport" (6). She is sure that had she remained in Europe she would still be "a thin flame on the mighty altar of Rome" (6). Beatrice has a drinking problem, a vice borrowed from Edward Fitzgerald, and she is charmed by Amory's experimentation with apricot cordial and cigarettes, a reaction that would have appalled Mollie Fitzgerald. Furthermore, the delicacy of Beatrice's features and the style and simplicity of her clothes are in marked contrast to the appearance of Mollie Fitzgerald.

Amory is as ambivalent about his mother as Fitzgerald was about his own. Beatrice's stylishness, sophistication, and beauty are sources of pride for Amory. However, her self-indulgence and weakness, which are evident in her drinking and hypochondria, and, most important, her permissiveness and failure to give her son

sound values account for Amory's cynicism, for even at five he had
no illusions about her. Her death is mentioned just in passing and
only in relation to Amory's growing financial problems. Beatrice's
extravagance and witless speculation in mass-transit companies
had depleted the considerable O'Hara fortune, and Amory is
especially annoyed that she left half of her meager estate to be
spent in endowments for stained-glass windows and seminaries in
"a sudden burst of religiosity." Amory speculates about whether
Beatrice had gone to heaven, and he concludes that she probably
did not, for she had had many love affairs. Amory is the only
representation of her immortality, and he is not impressed with her
legacy. In *This Side of Paradise* Fitzgerald worked out his own family
romance by creating for his fictional counterpart a mother who is
in many respects a wish fulfillment. Amory is, however, involved in
another aspect of the oedipal conflict, for his relationship with his
mother is essentially incestuous. Just as his mother encouraged
Fitzgerald, after his father's failures and relinquishment of his
paternal role, to assume the position of man of the family, so
Beatrice takes her young son as her consort. She encourages Amory
to call her Beatrice, and at age five he was "a delightful companion
for her" in their travels around the country in the O'Hara private
railroad car. Stephen Blaine is apparently estranged from Beatrice,
possibly because of either her love affairs or his absorption in
business matters. After his sojourn in Minneapolis, Amory joins his
parents at Lake Geneva, and Beatrice's behavior with her adolescent son can be described only as seductive.

> It was on one of the shadowy paths that Beatrice at last
> captured Amory. . . . After reproving him for avoiding her, she
> took him for a long tête-à-tête in the moonlight. He could not
> reconcile himself to her beauty, that was mother to his own,
> the exquisite neck and shoulders. . . . (20)

Obviously Amory had instinctively and wisely avoided Beatrice,
and he is saved from this spell of narcissism and eroticism only by
Beatrice's references to her prodigious drinking, her breakdowns,
and her lyrical description of an incidence of delirium tremens.
Amory snickers, and he is safely cynical about her again.

The father of this family is a shadowy figure who is more than faintly reminiscent of Edward Fitzgerald. (Stephen Blaine is named for St. Stephen the Martyr, a subtle detail which mitigates Fitzgerald's denunciatory portrait of him.) He is an ineffectual father, for he apparently is not interested enough in Amory to see or attempt to interfere in his wife's pathological handling of their son. Like Edward Fitzgerald, he has a taste for Byron, and he has a habit of drowsing over the *Encyclopaedia Britannica.* He is mentioned only a few times in the novel in relation either to his inept handling of the family's finances and the resultant adjustments Amory must make or to his death and funeral. Amory attends his father's funeral with an attitude of "amused tolerance," and the first bit of writing he sells is a cynical story about this experience. Obviously the oedipal impulse to kill the father is strong not only in Amory but also in his creator, for the death of the father figures in each Fitzgerald novel. Anthony Patch's father is dead, and his surrogate parent, his grandfather, is too much a part of the reformist movement of Anthony Comstock, for whom Anthony is named, to be sympathetic to the moral vacuity of his grandson.

The Patch family is a typical Fitzgerald invention. Anthony's mother, whom he remembers as the Boston Society contralto who sang for endless drawing rooms full of polite mannequins, "joined another choir" when he was five. His father is notable for being the first man in America to roll the lapels of his coat, and he is remembered by his son for his "thick-smelling words" in his visits to Anthony's nursery. A few years after Mrs. Patch's death, during their European tour, in the very best hotel in Lucerne, Mr. Patch died "with much sweating and grunting and crying aloud for air" (7). Anthony is obviously embarrassed by his father's lack of decorum, and this dispassionate memory reveals the son's true feeling for the father. Jay Gatsby figuratively kills his father when he denies his name and looks to Dan Cody as his surrogate father. The death of Dick Diver's father comes at a crucial time for him, when he recognizes that his marriage and identity are disintegrating, and it provides Dick an opportunity both literally and figuratively to step back from his life in Europe to view with shattering perspective his spiritual bankruptcy. The father of the hero of the Basil stories, the character Fitzgerald developed a decade after he had sketched it in Stephen Palms in "The Romantic Egoist," is also dead. None of Fitzgerald's characters mourns his dead father except Jacques Chandelle in "Shadow Laurels" (1915) and Dick Diver in *Tender Is the Night* (1934), who stand at either end of the continuum of Fitzgerald's attempts to come to terms with his ambivalence about his own father. It is telling that he was finally able to draw a mature and sympathetic portrait of a father only after his own was, in fact, dead.

The better father for Amory, ironically, is supplied him by his mother. Beatrice sends Amory to Monsignor Darcy, for she is sure that he will give to her son the same tender understanding he had given her in their youth. After Beatrice O'Hara had completed her European education and returned to this country, she had had a "clerical romance" with him which she now chooses to confess only to members of the hierarchy. The pagan Swinburnian young man in Asheville, a southerner like Edward Fitzgerald, whose passionate kisses and conversation she had found extremely attractive, did not have the proper background, and they consequently parted. Darcy went through a spiritual crisis, joined the Catholic Church, and became a monsignor and eventually the cardinal's right-hand man, while Beatrice, weary and saddened, had decided to marry Stephen Blaine because of his background and position. Both Beatrice and Darcy consider Amory their son somehow conceived in the transcendent spirituality of their love. Darcy tells Amory that he has enjoyed imagining that Amory is his son "begat" in some blessedly forgotten and comatose state in his youth, which echoes Fay's telling Fitzgerald that an explanation of their extraordinary relationship was that they were "a repetition of some common ancestor." [28] In just a half hour's conversation Amory and Darcy discover that they both favor the lost causes of Bonnie Prince Charlie, Hannibal, and the South, and adopt the respective roles of father and son.

The affectionate portrait of Darcy in *This Side of Paradise* grew out of Fitzgerald's love for Fay, and it expresses the combination of intellectual posing, snobbery, and the deep mutual concern which characterized their relationship. Darcy lives in a palatial mansion on the Hudson, which closely resembles the home of Margaret Chanler, the wealthy Catholic convert to whom Fay had introduced Fitzgerald and the original of Mrs. Lawrence in *This Side of Paradise*. Here Darcy lives between his trips to all parts of the Roman Catholic world like an exiled Stuart king waiting to be restored, just as young Scott Fitzgerald, rightful heir of the Stuart kings, had languished in St. Paul. In his purple regalia Darcy resembles a Turner sunset, a picture taken from Shane Leslie's description of Fay after his investiture as a monsignor. Darcy had written two novels, one anti-Catholic, the other anti-Episcopalian, parallels to the books Fay wrote before and after his conversion. Fitzgerald dedicated *This Side of Paradise* to his second father, and in the novel he used Fay's letters and a keen which Fay had written for him. Shane Leslie objected to this, and he and Father Hemmick reproved Fitzgerald for making Darcy and by implication his model, Monsignor Fay, a worldly, human figure. Leslie, who wrote a review of *This Side of Paradise* for the *Dublin Review*, actually an encomium of Fay which barely notices Fitzgerald, complained that Fitzgerald missed the "mystical note" in Fay; other writers in the Catholic press characterized the book as a subtle attack on the American clergy. Fitzgerald ignored this orthodox carping. Fay had been a loving and supportive father to him, and it was important that he record this in his first novel, which he called a somewhat edited history of himself and his imagination.

It was not only the portrait of Darcy but also Amory's confessions of doubt about Catholicism to which the Catholic critics objected. Though he had not been educated as a Catholic, Amory makes much at the end of the book of rejecting the religion his mother had observed only when her affectations and whims had moved her. The abolutism that is as strong in Amory as it was in Fitzgerald makes him demand perfection of Monsignor Darcy, and when he recognizes that this father is as fallible as his own, he reassesses Darcy's priestly character and finds it wanting. Amory observed that Darcy's faith had wavered at times, and this was both inexplicable and unforgivable to him. He concluded that this priest was not essentially older than he, and he was just a little wiser and somewhat purer. However, this rejection is more of Amory's posing; his disillusionment probably comes out of the child's natural resentment of a parent's deserting him in death.

This rejection is not complete, nor is it consistent with the affective account of Darcy's "magnificently Catholic and liturgical" funeral in which Fitzgerald used Shane Leslie's description of Monsignor Fay's funeral. That Amory considered Darcy his true father is evident in his "haunting grief" at his death, which is in marked contrast with the amused tolerance and cynicism with which he attends Stephen Blaine's funeral. Amory had leaned on Monsignor's faith, on his way "of making religion a thing of lights and shadows, making all light and shadow merely aspects of God" (266).

Several inconsistencies indicate that Amory's Catholic consciousness and the references in the book to things Catholic come out of Fitzgerald's experience rather than Amory's character. Amory's eccentric role-playing in his senior year at Princeton, his interest in mysticism, his reading *The Life of St. Theresa* while feigning a mystic daze are more truly related to Fitzgerald's life than Amory's. The frequent use of Catholic references in the novel is striking, especially in that they are meant to reflect the consciousness of a young man who admits that he is not even a Catholic and that he is "spiritually unmarried." Amory talks of Princeton campus figures as "holders of the apostolic succession" and of escaping finally to Mexico, where "he might live a strange litany, delivered from the hound of heaven" (262), a reference to the poem of that name written by the Catholic mystic, Francis Thompson, which fascinates Amory as it did Fitzgerald. And in his discussions of religion with his classmate, Burne Holiday, who is called Savonarola, Amory assumes the persona of Cardinal Richelieu and holds to the conservative Church position.

Just as Fitzgerald told Ginevra King that he intended to be a priest, so Amory tries to convince her counterpart, Rosalind, that he is a serious type by telling her that he is "religious." Amory sounds like a partisan when he suggests to his classmate, Tom D'Invilliers, that he would write better poetry if he were a Catholic linked to tall candlesticks and long, even chants. He also offers to introduce Tom to the "sporty churches" and to Monsignor Darcy, a priest who is not at all like the bourgeois American clergy to whom Beatrice had objected. Moreover, Amory's considering his Irishness a source of strength seems anomalous, for his mother's

superficial Catholic and Continental experience have not provided
the background Darcy describes for Amory. When Amory admits
that his Celtic traits were "pillars of his personal philosophy," it is
Fitzgerald speaking through him.

Just as Fitzgerald at Princeton was assiduously following
Monsignor Fay's reading list designed to safeguard him against
what Fay felt was Princeton's insidious Protestantism, so Amory
reads Benson, MacKenzie, Swinburne, Dowson, Wilde, all either
attracted to or converted to Catholicism. A book that deeply
impresses Amory is Harold Frederic's *The Damnation of Theron Ware*,
which Fitzgerald had read with interest and included in his
"College of One" curriculum for Sheilah Graham years later. It is
the story of a young Protestant minister's attraction to Catholicism, which is inspired by a small circle of Catholic intellectuals,
aesthetes who care more for beautiful ritual than for the fine points
of dogma. They discount the Church Fathers like Augustine for
their narrow asceticism, their emphasis on sin and hell fire, and
their disdain of women; and they are sympathetic to the Irish,
whom they consider the victims of their self-contradictory natures.
Theron is unceremoniously rejected by this group for his attempt
to be something he is not. Catholicism is a gift, according to
Frederic, and if it is not solely an accident of birth, then one must
have some inherent and mystical affinity for it. Theron does not
meet these requirements, but Amory and Fitzgerald do. This novel
reinforced the sense of privilege that Monsignor Fay was trying to
impress upon Fitzgerald, and Darcy upon Amory.

Edmund Wilson told Fitzgerald that the intellectual content
of *This Side of Paradise* was ludicrous, that Amory's mind was
shallow, and that his opinions were specious. It is difficult not to
agree with Wilson, considering Amory's political naiveté and his
anomalous religious opinions. His brief association with Monsignor
Darcy is hardly enough preparation for the fact that religion
means only the Church of Rome to him and his acceptance of it as
"the only assimilative traditionary bulwark against the decay of
morals" (281). As the book ends we know little about what he will
make of his life. He proclaims himself part of the new generation
that has "grown up to find all Gods dead, all wars fought, all faiths
in man shaken" (282), and although there is no God in his heart

and his ideas are still tenuous, he thinks that art, politics, or religion might be the medium for the expression of the fundamental Amory, "the idle, imaginative, rebellious" essential self which is the only thing of which he is certain. The fact that religion should occur to Amory as one of the channels for his energies and that Catholicism has claimed an inordinate portion of his consciousness belies the contention of some that *This Side of Paradise* marks Fitzgerald's conclusive break with the Church. Amory says that total acceptance of Catholicism is impossible for the present, after all, not for all time. It is true that within a few years after the publication of *This Side of Paradise,* Fitzgerald was no longer canonically a Catholic; but, like Amory Blaine, he was never able totally to shed the residual effects of his Catholicism.

What makes *This Side of Paradise* essentially the product of Fitzgerald's Catholic consciousness is not so much the character of Monsignor Darcy, Amory's preoccupation with the appearances of Catholicism, and the book's Catholic language, but rather Amory's profound sense of evil and especially his association of evil with sexuality and feminine beauty which had descended to him from Augustine through ages of repressive Church teaching. Fitzgerald said that his mother, his wife, and his last sweetheart are all one woman to a man, and all of the women in the novel, excluding the ethereal Clara, are embodiments of evil for Amory, for whom "the problem of evil had solidified . . . into the problem of sex" (280), which is inseparably linked with beauty. In reviewing his situation, Amory concludes that every time he had reached toward beauty longingly, "it had leered out at him with the grotesque face of evil" (280). The women in his life have been masked destroyers, beginning with Beatrice, whose charm and deceptively youthful beauty mask the dangerous and debilitating feelings for Amory that he knows instinctively he must avoid.

The second female in Amory's life is Myra St. Claire, the young Golden Girl of Amory's Minneapolis phase, who closely resembles Basil's Gladys Van Schellinger. Unlike Basil with Gladys, Amory is on an equal financial footing with Myra, another significant wish-fulfilling alteration Fitzgerald made in the biographical material of this novel. When Amory contrives to be alone

with Myra at a country-club party, he represents himself as a blasé
and daring male, but, when his posing forces the situation to a
crisis, his reaction is incongruous. Alone with Myra in the den
before the fireplace, in the most romantic and advantageous
situation with a compliant partner, Amory kisses her and immediately lapses into a paroxysm of guilt, like Augustine who
scourged himself for his impulse to "scratch at the itching sore of
lust."

> Sudden revulsion seized Amory, disgust, loathing for the
> whole incident. He desired frantically to be away, never to see
> Myra again, never to kiss any one . . . he wanted to creep out
> of his body and hide somewhere safe out of sight, up in the
> corner of his mind. (14)

This young Adam, burdened by his sexuality, the original sin, who
tastes "his lips curiously as if he had munched some new fruit"
(14), enticed to a new and frightening awareness, stares at the
temptress as if she were a new species of animal of whose existence
he had not been aware. Amory's overreaction to this kiss,
reminiscent of Basil's revulsion at the painted young destroyer in
"A Night at the Fair," is surely abnormal, an indication of Amory's
disturbed sexuality. His puritan conscience, his desire, however, to
influence others even for evil, and especially his furtive interest in
everything concerning sex comprise the essential Amory hiding
behind his sophisticated mask.

In the section devoted to "Petting," which partly accounted
for the book's reputation, Amory, supposedly the prototypical
"flaming youth," speaks out of his puritan conscience of the "real
moral letdown" he has seen in his cross-country tour with the
Princeton Triangle Club. The Popular Daughter who scandalizes
him eats "three-o'clock after-dance suppers in impossible cafés,
disappears between dances, if met before eight might be kissed
before twelve" (59). First the "belle" she has become the "flirt" and
then the "baby vamp." However, in his associations with the
"P.D.," Amory tires her with his habit of analyzing every situation,
and he is less a participant in this cultural phenomenon than its
historian.

Amory is still the poseur with the next woman in his life, Isabelle, the counterpart of Ginevra King and the transplanted heroine of the 1917 story, "Babes in the Woods." He is a sophomore at Princeton, and she is the cousin of a Minneapolis friend who is visiting from the South for the Christmas holiday. They meet as practiced adversaries in a war game that is both an escalation of the incident with Myra and an anticipation of the campaigns with Rosalind and Eleanor. Amory matches Isabelle's vanity, narcissism, and wiles, and when she uses the artificial walk she had created as a child and plays the starry-eyed ingenue, Amory, who knows as well as she every nuance of the game, is not deceived. "He waited for the mask to drop off, but at the same time he did not question her right to wear it!" (66). She, on the other hand, is not impressed by his practiced air of sophisticiation, but she respects his skill and accepts his pose. This parrying runs its course as they advance to a final confrontation in the den, the scene of his peculiar reaction to Myra St. Claire's kiss. Amory asks for a memento, and with the same deliberateness Myra had displayed in her seduction scene, Isabelle calmly tells Amory to close the door, after which much is made of an unconsummated kiss. A line from a song, "Babes in the Woods," an ironic comment on the participants in this charade, which floats in from an adjoining room, suggests the Catholic orientation that is more nearly Basil's and Fitzgerald's than Amory's, and which helps to explain Amory's habitual squeamishness—"Fourteen angels watching o'er them" (71).

Fitzgerald is not titillating the reader here; rather one senses that there is a profound revulsion to expressions of sexuality in him that surfaces in this sort of fictional situation. Some months later when Isabelle and Amory meet during a seemingly perfect college weekend, their war game resumes with the completion of that kiss begun in the den. When Amory inadvertently stabs Isabelle on the neck with his shirt stud, the tables are turned on this vampire, and she is marked by the sign of her type. This violation of her appearance angers her inordinately, and their relationship takes an ugly turn. What tenderness Amory had felt for Isabelle is dispelled by her rage, and her refusal to kiss him becomes an issue in which he must prevail. It would worry him if he could not kiss her, for it would deflate his image of himself as a conqueror; he would not be second best and plead with a valiant warrior like Isabelle. Amory daringly pushes the situation to a crisis with his ultimatum that they kiss or nothing. Isabelle refuses and confesses her boredom and fatigue at his endless analysis of every emotion and instinct. Amory admits to this tendency, but he recovers his composure with the rationalization that he had created the wonder of Isabelle in his imagination and that by falling short of his phantasm she had spoiled his year.

The carnival section of the novel, which begins in innocence and youthful joy and culminates in death and a horrible vision of sin involving a woman, and which contributes to Amory's deepening awareness of sorrow, is appropriately interwined with his experience with Isabelle. Fitzgerald carried over the Devil section from "The Romantic Egoist" manuscript essentially unchanged, but in *This Side of Paradise* it is effectively prepared for in two earlier episodes. "Original Sin," as Amory is called by his Princeton friends, an epithet that indicates his essential seriousness and sexual fastidiousness, is induced to join the others in a springtime romp at the beach. It is all boyish exuberance and great fun from which Amory stands a bit apart in his customary habit of analyzing people and situations, for his participation in revelry is prurient rather than licentious, and he is especially impressed by and envious of Dick Humbird's social ease. Several weeks later another excursion, this time to a party in New York, is cruelly punctuated by an accident on the way back to Princeton in which Humbird is killed. This is Amory's first intimate experience with death, and it is a glimpse of the horrible underside of the carnival that life had been for him. The striking charm and personality of Humbird are reduced to a grotesque and squalid "heavy white mass," and for the first time Amory is aware of his own mortality.

The Devil episode occurs during another Dionysian revel in New York. It begins in a cafe filled with Broadway characters and women of questionable character. Amory hopes that his evening will end harmlessly, but he feels that some hostile force is plotting to strip Broadway of its romance in a way so terrible that the experience will indelibly mark him for life. As Amory's classmate

and the girls they are with become increasingly more intoxicated
and abandoned, he remains soberly analytical. Before their party
moves on to the apartment of one of the girls, Amory notices that
an incongruous figure in this crowd, a middle-aged man in a
brown sack suit, is staring at him. Amory appoints himself his
friend's protector, and he hopes that he does not sound priggish in
his suggestion that they hurry the evening to a safe conclusion.
Shortly after they enter the apartment, however, there is a moment
when temptation envelops him and he decides to give himself over
to the mood of the others. But as Basil had seen the joy of carnival
transformed into the horror of the hell-mouth, Amory sees across
the room the man from the cafe. His pallor is strange, as if he had
done much underground work, and suddenly Amory notices his
feet—he wears pointed moccasins instead of shoes and his toes seem
to fill them to the ends. The others cannot see the Devil, but
Amory clearly perceives that the couch that held the man "was
alive . . . like heat waves over asphalt, like wriggling worms" (114).
Disturbed especially by the figure's feet, Amory rushes from the
apartment into the street below where he senses that he is pursued.
He realizes suddenly that the footsteps are ahead of him and that
he is actually following them. Amory darts into a blind alley and
in terror waits for the figure to confront him. A pale face distorted
with evil flashes before his eyes, and he knows for that half instant
that it is the face of Dick Humbird, who had come to mean to him
the horrible reality of the carnival or the City of Man—his own
temporality and mortality.

The nightmarish carnival does not end with the night,
however. The glorious May morning following this darkest night is
a cruel contrast to Amory's moral hangover, and the "babel of
noise and the painted faces" (177) he meets on Broadway, now
tawdry in daylight, sicken him. In the hotel barber shop the smell
of powders and tonics, materials with which to construct a mask,
make him recall the chorus girls' suggestive smiles, and on the train
back to Princeton a painted woman across the aisle sickens him.
Amory's roommate, Tom D'Invilliers, greets him with the news
that he had dreamed the night before about Amory being in
trouble, but Amory refuses to talk about his experience and tries to
recover his equilibrium by reading Wells and Rupert Brooke. A

storm comes up, and at a lightning flash, Tom stares transfixed at
the window where he sees something staring at Amory. The Devil,
who perceives Amory's vulnerability and sees in him a likely
protégé, will continue to stalk him.

Amory forgets this horror for a time in his friendship with
Clara Page, a fond portrait of Fitzgerald's cousin, Cecelia Taylor.
Her "immemorial" beauty of person and character set her above
the other women in the book, and Amory thinks of her as the first
fine woman he has known. Clara, who is a third cousin he never
knew existed, is introduced to Amory by Monsignor Darcy, a point
which helps to establish her moral perfection. She is a young
widow with small children who were apparently somehow mirac-
ulously born to her; she claims she has never been in love, and
Amory approaches her "with almost the realization that Joseph
must have had of Mary's eternal significance" (145). Clara is the
perfect woman; she has a "calm virility," she is level-headed,
intellectual, a delightful raconteur—qualities usually considered
masculine ones. Most important, her deep spirituality and her
golden radiance, which at times make her seem to be a disem-
bodied spirit, make her unapproachable. No man is good enough
for her, according to Amory, a remarkable admission for this
supreme egotist. He tells Clara that he loves—or adores—or
worships her, each word taking him farther from consummation of
his emotion.

On one of his weekend trips to Philadelphia to visit Clara,
Amory goes with her to church where he watches her kneeling and
bending her golden hair into the stained-glass light, and he
involuntarily cries aloud, "St. Cecelia!" In a love poem he writes
for her he assigns this persona to Clara, and he tells her that if he
were to lose faith in her he would lose his faith in God. Amory
begins to speculate wildly about marriage, but he knows that this
desire is not sincere. He had dreamed once that they had married
and he had awakened in a cold panic, for in his dream the golden
Clara was brazen. This Poe-like interlude in Amory's education in
the ways of Woman shows that he cannot relate in an elemental
way to a flesh-and-blood woman who is not a destroyer. He tells
Clara wistfully that she would have been a consummate devil "if

the Lord had just bent her soul a little the other way" (146). But this Helen is purity incarnate and unattainable—just the way Amory would have it. This side of paradise, such a love is impossible.

Rosalind Connage is an amplified, more fully drawn version of the heroine of Fitzgerald's 1917 one-act play *The Debutante*. She is the prototypical flapper, the sort of vampire who smokes, drinks, is frequently kissed, and who treats cruelly all men who adore her. Even before Rosalind meets Amory she questions her brother, Alec, about his financial status, and with this another dimension is added to Fitzgerald's portrait of the female destroyer—her demand that the man who will win her be rich. Fifty-one shares in "Rosalind, Unlimited . . . name, good will, everything goes at $25,000 a year" (174), she tells Amory. But she is not exactly calculating about money; "she never *thinks* about money," rather her nature simply requires it for her emotional well-being. This facet of Fitzgerald's portrait of Rosalind reflects his view of Zelda, who had broken their engagement just before he set to work on *This Side of Paradise*. He saw money as the first issue between them, as he thought it had been between him and Ginevra King, and the demand for wealth had become firmly established in his concept of the desirable woman. For the first time, Amory forgets his egoism and falls in love, for Rosalind's vanity and selfishness cannot overshadow her enthusiasm, her will to grow, her endless faith in romance, and her courage and essential honesty—qualities Fitzgerald loved in Zelda.

Amory and Rosalind meet in her dressing room, and she shows him the devices, the rouge and eye pencils with which she constructs her mask, which she uses in both a defensive and aggressive way. Rosalind says that she must "keep [her] face like steel . . . to keep men from winking at [her]" (172), and she uses her mask featuring an "eternal kissable mouth" in her frontal attacks in her sexual war games. After they kiss, Amory exclaims "Lord help me," and Rosalind declares that "the war is over" and that "the Home-team has won." Amory is thoroughly and miserably involved in a love that is a "paradise of rose and flame," a relationship of both unearthly beauty and hellish suffering. For several weeks Amory works for a pittance in an advertising agency by day and each night tries to persuade Rosalind to marry him. She tells him that they would soon hate each other in a marriage of poverty and struggle, and she sends him away with the final cruel news that she will marry another, wealthy suitor. Amory had been able to put aside his sexual squeamishness in his love for Rosalind, but the consummation of that love is prevented by still another problem out of Fitzgerald's experience—the problem of money and its intimate involvement in sexual relationships.

Amory meets Eleanor Savage, an apt surname for this wild and curious creature, shortly after his crisis with Rosalind. Eleanor is less a woman than the embodiment of the evil that is Woman, *la belle dame sans merci,* for she is "the last time that evil crept close to Amory under the mask of beauty" (222). Keats was Fitzgerald's favorite poet, and in the Eleanor episode he is indebted to the theme and tone of "La Belle Dame Sans Merci." Amory wanders like Keats's knight-at-arms, sleepless and woe-begone, in a melancholy, autumnal landscape where he meets the mysterious wild-eyed Eleanor singing Verlaine to an extemporaneous tune, just as Keats's Lady of the meads sings a faery's song. The place where they meet "seemed fairyland ... with dim phantasmal shapes, expressing eternal beauty and curious elfin love moods" (233)—it is Keats's elfin grot. Eleanor is Amory's alter ego; her Continental mother had raised her in the cavalier fashion of Beatrice Blaine; she is Irish; she has green eyes; she has an uncanny way of reading Amory's thoughts; and they spend their last night on horseback like Keats's elfin lovers after an enchanted week together. As they ride, they discuss, among other things, sex, and it seems that she is as troubled about it as Amory, who pompously expounds on the subject. Intellectuals, he says, cover it up by pretending it has nothing to do with their "shining brains," but he admits that intellect is no protection from sex, which finds its way into the midst of one's purest abstractions. Eleanor attacks his hypocrisy and reveals the actual source of his and her own disturbed sexuality.

Oh, you're just an old hypocrite, too. Thousands of scowling priests keeping the degenerate Italians and illiterate

Irish repentant with gabble-gabble about the sixth and ninth commandments. It's all just cloaks, sentimental and spiritual rouge ... and you're too much the prig to admit it. ... (239

Amory's materialism is torn to shreds by what he terms Eleanor's blasphemy, and he angrily imputes to her the hypocrisy of which she has accused him: "like Napoleon and Oscar Wilde and the rest of your type," he asserts, "you'll yell loudly for a priest on your death-bed" (239). She attempts to kill herself by riding her horse over a cliff to disprove Amory's charge, and the elfin charm is broken as dawn comes. Their poses are scattered like broken glass in the pale dawn, and Amory sees that as he had loved himself in Eleanor there is much in both of them that is hateful.

In the section titled "The Supercilious Sacrifice," immediately after his interlude with Eleanor, Amory goes to Atlantic City both to luxuriate in self-pity over the loss of Rosalind, whom he has been unable to forget, and to recall the riotous Carnival by the Sea of four years before, the spring trip to Asbury Park. The thesis of this and all of his bad nights in his painfully learned cynical conviction that a woman has to appeal to the worst in him to hold a man. Then, as if to confirm his mood and the fact that "the worst" in man is his sexuality, Alec Connage, Rosalind's brother and one of Amory's companions on the earlier happy and innocent trip to the sea, turns up with Jill, a "gaudy, vermilion-lipped blonde." They arrange for Amory to take the adjoining room at Alec's hotel, and he continues his solitary and melancholy reminiscence. Later that night Amory is awakened by house detectives pounding on the door and Alec's and Jill's alarmed entreaties for help. Alec has violated the Mann Act by bringing Jill to Atlantic City, and Amory decides to help him by taking the blame himself. It seems to him that an open scroll is flung before him on which is written the meaning of such sacrifice—power and the risk of ruin and despair, the arrogance, impersonality, and eternal superciliousness that are the nature of sacrifice.

But Amory is suddenly aware of other presences in the room. A horrible aura broods over them while another strangely familiar shape makes its protective presence known. The Devil thus makes his second appearance in the novel. Here he is the awesome aura appropriately focused on the painted woman on the bed who tempts Amory to yield to cynicism. But the figure by the window utters the words "Weep not for me but for thy children," the words the supreme sacrificer, Jesus, spoke to his despairing followers as he was being scourged on the way to Calvary. Amory thinks that this is the way God would talk to him, and he feels a great surge of joy. The aura over the bed fades: the shadow by the window lingers a moment longer and then is lifted from the room by a breeze. Days later Amory learns that Monsignor Darcy had died on that night, and then he knows what presence had saved him from despair. With the girl, he faces the house detectives, but he escapes ruin when the hotel decides not to prosecute them.

Amory's joy in his selfless sacrifice is short-lived, however. Back in New York, which had become an inferno for him after his earlier midnight confrontation with the Devil, Amory realizes that his salvation had been merely temporary. Even though he espouses their cause in his naive discourse on socialism, he is no Christlike champion of the poor, whom he considers coarse, dirty, and stupid. In fact, Amory concedes the possibility that he might join the Devil's legion: "What if some day ... he became a thing that frightened children and crept into rooms in the dark, approached dim communion with those phantoms who whispered shadowy secrets to the mad of that dark continent upon the moon?" (261). At the end of his quest and his novel, Amory knows himself but that is all, and what he is firmly convinced of is his infinite capacity for evil. *This Side of Paradise* was hailed in its time as a document of youthful revolt, but it is more nearly a case history of the pathology of one young man's soul. And instead of easing Amory's sickness, the women he has known have only contributed to his malaise, for their beauty, which he had hoped to transmute into modes of art, has given him only a sick heart and a few puzzled words to write.

Shortly after *This Side of Paradise* was published, Mrs. James J. Hill, the wife of the railroad king, one of Fitzgerald's heroes, told a St. Paul bookseller, "I've been looking for someone to write the life of Archbishop Ireland and now I think I've found him. They tell me there is a fine young Catholic writer who has just published a religious book, *This Side of Paradise*." [29] This statement, apparently ludicrously naive in the context of the time and life of Scott Fitzgerald, was uncanny in its characterization of Fitzgerald's first novel. For all its appeal to flaming youth in the 1920s and its apparent unorthodoxy, *This Side of Paradise* is actually the product of a deeply religious sensibility. In another time and place, its author probably would have been tried for heresy—not, as one might conclude on the basis of its reputation, for unorthodoxy and licentiousness—but, as was the case for Savanarola, for excessive scrupulousness. *This Side of Paradise,* the keystone for the understanding of his themes and characterizations, is the primer among Fitzgerald's works, and it is not incidental that it is the most overtly Catholic novel in his canon.

3.

The Sad Young Man: 1920-1924

Fitzgerald was most concerned with the response of two audiences to his first novel: the young who embraced *This Side of Paradise* as their manifesto, and the Church, which was not so enthusiastic. He wrote to Shane Leslie:

> If you knew the absolute dirth [sic] of Catholic intelligentsia in this country! One Catholic magazine, *America,* had only one prim comment on my book—"a fair example of our non-Catholic college's [sic] output." My Lord! Compared to the average Georgetown alumnus Amory is an uncanonized saint. I think I laundered myself shiny in the book! [1]

Leslie replied that Catholics never recognize their own "bred and born genius" and urged him to be patient,[2] advice that was gratuitous, for the new direction Fitzgerald's life took after his marriage and his success inevitably led him away from the influence of Leslie and the Church.

The Fitzgeralds' fame in the early 1920s was a phenomenon attributable to the riotous temper of that time, the Fitzgeralds' affinity for a frenetic life-style, and their innate genius for the art of press agentry. Their natural exuberance and sense of the outlandish was usually enough to keep them in the public eye; their dip in the Plaza fountain, riding on the roofs of taxicabs, stripping at a

Scandals performance, and dancing on restaurant tables managed to gain them considerable attention. But one week when they had not made the papers, probably when they were recovering from one of their peripatetic marathon parties, Fitzgerald did hand-stands in the Biltmore lobby to ensure a notice. To escape the dissolution of the New York whirl, the Fitzgeralds rented a house in Connecticut, but their friends transported the New York hysteria to the country every weekend. Just as Fitzgerald had been appalled by his Princeton classmates' casual sexual encounters, when he was roused to jealousy over his wife, the old-fashioned morality of his puritanical upbringing surfaced and precipitated rifts between them. And for all his desire to please, to amuse his guests with endless entertainments, the moralist in Fitzgerald secretly worried about working to support their extravagance rather than his dream of being the best young American writer.

After three months of unquiet marriage he found himself in debt, and although he was working hard on his second novel, *The Beautiful and Damned,* he set to work to produce enough magazine fiction just to meet their exorbitant current expenses. But the seriousness of much of the writing of this period and Fitzgerald's self-revelatory statements show that his gaiety was superficial and that he stood back to observe critically his own and his contempo-raries' restless behavior. In his essay "Early Success" he talks about the relief and abandon they felt after the war. Yet beneath the riotous life of this cynosure of the Jazz Age there was an insidious deterministic presentiment that they were all doomed. All of the stories he thought of writing had a touch of disaster in them, for his diamond mountains blew up and his millionaires were damned. Fitzgerald was sure that living was not the careless business they all thought it was.

"The Diamond as Big as the Ritz," [3] at one level a mar-velously whimsical fantasy, was written during this time, and it clearly demonstrates that Fitzgerald was aware of the seriousness beneath its tawdry appearances. The several curious Christian references in the story indicate also that the "old Catholic" in Fitzgerald had much to do with its composition. All of the humorous and analogic possibilities of the name of John T. Unger's midwestern home town, Hades, are noted by Fitzgerald—

the homefires kept burning for John, the asbestos pocketbook he is given by his father, the town's oppressive heat, and the depressing Dantesque motto hanging over the city gates which is strangely evocative for John. The advice his father gives him, not to forget who he is and where he comes from, and his being intrigued and readily impressed by the appearances of wealth make him a predecessor of Nick Carraway; and he, too, is a chronicler of what he meets in the mysterious East.

Because his parents, like all prosperous parents in Hades, feel that their son must have the advantage of a New England education, John is sent to St. Midas' School near Boston, an ironic parallel to Fitzgerald's Newman School and Basil's St. Regis, where he is by comparison with the others a poor boy in a rich boys' school. In his second year he meets Percy Washington, an aloof and extremely wealthy boy even by St. Midas' standard. Percy tells John that his father is the richest man in the world, and John eagerly accepts his invitation to spend the summer with him at his home in the West, declaring that he likes rich people and, in fact, that the richer a fellow is the better he likes him. In reply to John's rhapsodic account of the fabulous jewels he has seen at the homes of other St. Midas boys and his own modest cache he had collected instead of stamps, Percy announces that his father owns a diamond bigger that the Ritz-Carlton Hotel, which stuns John into reverent silence. The first leg of the journey ends at the Montana village named Fish, an obvious Christian allusion, and here the boys are met by a group of twelve somber and mysterious men who are like a strange race apart created by some whim and then left to struggle and extermination. They meet each night at seven at the depot, and their sole purpose seems to be to observe, with a marked absence of wonder and enthusiastic expectancy, the emergence of the passengers of the train, brought to a stop here a few times a year by the Great Brakeman. The savior never arrives, and these latter-day counterparts of the apostles acting out their absurd mission in this godless, secular City of Man, drift away with no hint of even the passion of disappointment.

John is properly awed by the fantastic circus wagon of a car which carries them far into the mountains to the Washington homestead, for he has learned well the simple piety of Hades, which holds as the first article of its creed the worship and respect of riches. He knows he is about his Father's business and that He would have been appalled by John's blasphemy if he were not humble in the presence of such opulence. Percy sketches in his family's background, that he is a direct descendant of George Washington and that his family had followed the American prescription for success and adventurous ingenuity to its corrupt end by building the greatest fortune in the world on the ruin of others. As a young man his grandfather had discovered a diamond mountain, anonymously amassed his fortune, and then returned to his secret kingdom. Of course, he had had to kill his own brother, but very few other murders had marred these good years of progress and expansion. Using the godly power of his wealth, he had corrupted the state survey department, altered the official federal maps, deflected a river, and set up the facade of a village on its banks in order to protect his secret. The only violation of his kingdom has been the reconnaissance flights of adventuresome aviators, but some have been killed and others have been captured with antiaircraft guns. John's moral training has not equipped him to make a right judgment of the corrupt Washingtons, for, instead of being horrified at this history, he adheres to his father's religion in his rapt appreciation of the utter luxury of this place described in images out of a boy's dream of an earthly, materialistic paradise.

In the Arcadian landscape created by a film scenic designer, John meets and falls in love with Kismine, Percy's younger sister and a deceptively sweet destroyer. The sinister reality of this seemingly idyllic place surfaces with his glimpse of the perverse merry-go-round which imprisons errant aviators and the news that all visitors have been executed when their usefulness was at an end. On the night of his escape, the mountain fortress is invaded from the air, and before Mr. Washington detonates his kingdom rather than face a diminished life, John observes a curious ritual. Washington, "king and priest of the age of gold" (34), brings to the mountaintop an enormous diamond and condescendingly and arrogantly offers it as a bribe to God, who, made in the image of man, he thinks must have his price. He will build the most magnificent cathedral the world has seen and there offer in sacrifice any victim the Divine Benefactor should choose. But

God's price has not been met, and He gives His answer in the darkened sky and menacing thunder. John faces life with Kismine in Hades, chastened by his experience, which has deteriorated from dream to nightmare. He has seen the apotheosis of his father's creed and its explosion, and he will settle for a form of "divine drunkenness," loving Kismine for a year or two, and the knowledge that he will probably make nothing of his disillusion.

The artist in Fitzgerald required that he participate as completely as his energy and conscience would allow in the abandonment which marked the Roaring Twenties, but the moralist in him was ever censorious. In a few quiet moments of escape from a riotous evening, he told an acquaintance that "Parties are a form of suicide. I love them, but the old Catholic in me secretly disapproves." [4] This hard core of Fitzgerald's character, his midwestern puritanism or middle-class Catholicism, was his salvation, as burdensome as it might have been at times. It was, as Malcolm Cowley has said, what kept him from denying his obligation to his family and his artistic integrity. [5] This ambivalence in Fitzgerald has been termed his "spoiled-priest" posture, the view of one who has fallen from the state or the possibility of grace, whose essential double nature will not allow him totally to forget the quest for moral perfection or the impossibility of achieving it. The spoiled priest is, on the one hand, analytical, detached, and judgmental, and on the other, sympathetic to the impulse to transgress in himself and in others. The City of Man—City of God dichotomy in Fitzgerald's work is the thematic projection of his self-confessed spoiled-priest posture. It was the priest in him which effected Fitzgerald's comment about parties and his essential distrust of the money-making process, while the sybarite was creating his reputation as a prodigious host and guest and was driving him to amass and expend as much money as he could.

His moralism also partially prompted his writing of his second novel, *The Beautiful and Damned.* [6] Buried in the profusion of incident and philosophizing of this novel is a short section in which its hero, Anthony Patch, supports his resolve never to marry with the story of Chevalier O'Keefe, a wild Irishman exiled to France in the last days of chivalry. He has one weakness, his enormous susceptibility to all sorts of women. He is sentimental, romantic, vain, and a little blind in one eye and stoneblind in the other, the physical correlative of his moral state. He had been made miserable for twenty years by several women "who hated him, used him, bored him, aggravated him, sickened him, spent his money, made a fool of him—in brief, as the world has it, loved him" (90). To save himself, O'Keefe goes to the monastery of St. Voltaire, where he must spend the rest of his life in prayer and contemplation in one of the monastery's four towers named for the commandments of the Augustinian rule—poverty, chastity, obedience, and silence. For the first time he feels safe from his own sexuality as he starts up to his cell at the top of the tower of Chastity, and he pauses for a moment by an open window to drink in for the last time the beauty of the world he is leaving. Just then a passing peasant girl stops to adjust her garter, and as she lifts her skirt, O'Keefe, magnetically drawn by what he is trying to escape, leans from the window until a stone loosens under him, and he tumbles to "the hard earth and eternal damnation" (91). Because he is suspected of suicide, O'Keefe is not buried in consecrated ground, and the peasant girl spends ten years in secret penance and prayer for the soul of the monk whose neck and vows were broken simultaneously. The application of this parable to Fitzgerald's life is clear: the maxim that women make men miserable by their debilitating love and by keeping them from achieving their ideals, and actually destroy men through the allure of beauty and base sensuality, is the major theme of both Fitzgerald's life and work.

The would-be monk found himself a prospective father barely a year after his marriage. In May 1921, the Fitzgeralds went abroad for a two-month holiday before temporarily settling into parenthood and domesticity. In a letter to an American monsignor in Rome, which praises Fitzgerald's family as "staunch, devout, generous" supporters of the Church, Archbishop Austin Dowling of St. Paul spoke of Fitzgerald's great desire to see the Pope during his visit to Rome, and Dowling asked for his help in arranging the papal audience.[7] There is, however, no evidence that it ever took place. The trip was disappointing. France was not congenial; the Fitzgeralds hated the Italians and their country; and London was stuffy. They were not too unhappy this time to return to America, and after a month in Zelda's home town, they decided to go to St. Paul for the birth of their child.

Whenever Fitzgerald had returned to St. Paul—during his 1916 sabbatical from Princeton, in the summer of 1919 when he was writing *This Side of Paradise,* and in this 1921-22 sojourn—one of the people he saw regularly at the Kilmarnock Bookshop, the headquarters of local and visiting literati, was Father Joseph Thomas Barron, the last priest in his life. Fitzgerald's acquaintance with Joe Barron had begun years before when Barron's parish priest brought him to meet the influential McQuillans. Fitzgerald's senior by eight years, Barron became a close friend of Phillip McQuillan, Fitzgerald's uncle and godfather, and through this association came to know Fitzgerald in later years.

Joseph Barron came from a typical family of St. Paul, a predominantly Catholic city which had been built up by the migration of working-class Catholics from the East. His father, John Barron, had left Prince Edward Island for Minneapolis in the mid-nineteenth century. Many young people before him had gone to the St. Paul area either to study for the priesthood or to join the Carondelet of St. Joseph, a teaching order of nuns who were then important and powerful in St. Paul Church life. It was a tradition that vacationing clergy brought back with them more young Canadians to carry on their work, but while John Barron knew several of the priests and they influenced his move, he did not consider the priesthood for himself. His father had been a farmer, and with his move to the West, congruent with the growing spirit of industrialization, John Barron left the land for employment with a wholesale grocery firm in St. Paul, a branch of commerce dominated by Irish Catholics and which had been the source of the McQuillan prosperity.

In Minneapolis John Barron met Anne Boulger, a native Minnesotan, and a few years after their marriage they moved across the Mississippi River to St. Paul, where they raised their seven children in a deeply religious home.[8] Joseph Barron did not come from a long line of clergy; he was the first priest in his family. A brilliant student, he was soon noticed by the pastor for whom he served mass, and his parents were approached with the suggestion that he enter St. Paul Seminary. None of the Barrons had even remotely considered the possibility, but they were not opposed to the idea, and apparently Joe had a genuine vocation.[9] He studied at St. Thomas College and the Seminary in St. Paul, and when he was consecrated by Archbishop John Ireland in 1912 he was just twenty-four, the youngest priest ever to have been ordained in that diocese. Barron was immediately named dean of students at St. Paul Seminary, and thus began a distinguished academic career which took him to Catholic University, where he earned the degree of doctor of sacred theology and eventually joined the faculty. At his untimely death in 1939, Barron was dean of sacred theology and was known as one of the most brilliant students and teachers contributed to Catholic University by the Diocese of St. Paul, which had been instrumental in the establishment of the school.[10] One of this three books, *The Elements of Epistemology* (1931), has become a standard theology text widely used in Catholic seminaries and universities. His other works are *The Idea of the Absolute in Modern British Philosophy* (1929) and *Supplement to Turner's History of Philosophy* (1930).[11]

The tall, athletic priest, with his Irish good looks, blue eyes, and wavy red hair, was handsome in the style of the Arrow collar advertisements of that day, and he was a great favorite of his students. Not only was he a brilliant and stimulating teacher, but his disciplining of students was tempered by his delightful sense of humor. He was extremely proud to have received a facial scar, quickly healed, while playing hockey with his students, and he wore the plaster on his cheek like a decoration.[12] Fitzgerald, the thwarted football hero, was naturally attracted to this personality.

In the winter of 1916, Fitzgerald often visited Father Barron, who was then a curate at St. Paul Cathedral.[13] These visits were renewed when Fitzgerald returned to St. Paul in 1919, when John Briggs, later headmaster of St. Paul Academy, and Donald Stewart, a young writer whom Fitzgerald had encouraged in his work and introduced to the works of Catholic writers, often went with him to see Barron, in his rooms at St. Paul Seminary, where he was professor of philosophy. They discussed Fitzgerald's writing as well as other literary and religious matters, and it was probably then that Barron gave "Benediction" his imprimatur, as Fitzgerald later told Shane Leslie.

Barron was as alarmed as Monsignor Fay had been by Fitzgerald's spiritual instability, but his approach was gentle scorn rather than the emotional appeals the older fatherly priest had made. Barron was more nearly Fitzgerald's contemporary, and his natural response to Fitzgerald's iconoclasms was a quiet "Scott, quit being a damn fool." [15] Still Fitzgerald went back for more intellectual fencing with Father Barron, for he was impressed with the priest's keen intelligence, the breadth and depth of his learning, and his idealistic devotion to his students and teaching. But this association did not quiet Fitzgerald's spiritual turmoil. That his feelings about the Church were ambivalent, intense, and sometimes burdensome is evident in the report of a curious incident which occurred shortly before the birth of his daughter. His marriage to Zelda was a little more than a year old, and it was not going as well as it could. She was uncomfortable in St. Paul; being married to Zelda was not the bliss Fitzgerald had anticipated; and he had periods of depression. His momentary despair and the object of his anger were noted by a friend who thought it significant. They drove past a Catholic church one night, and Fitzgerald was heard to mutter, "God damn the Catholic Church; God damn the Church; God damn God!" [16]

Even though he was about to leave the Church, Fitzgerald arranged, at his mother's suggestion, to have his daughter baptized, and Father Barron was both the celebrating priest and Scottie's godfather. When it came time to christen the baby, there was a dispute between her parents about the name. Zelda favored the name Patricia. The only name Scott considered was Francis Scott Fitzgerald, sure that the child would be a boy, and he was at a loss until the nuns told him that he could use the name for a girl by changing the *i* to *e* in Francis. F. Scott Fitzgerald she was, and Scott told them, "If she is cute, we will call her Scottie." [17] Annabel, Scott's sister, was the baby's godmother, though she was not allowed to hold the child. Because of Fitzgerald's unpredictability, his mother wanted the ceremony conducted on a low key. Zelda did not attend the service.[18]

In the 1930s, when Fitzgerald's parents had moved to Washington, D.C., and the younger Fitzgeralds were living in Delaware and Maryland, Father Barron was teaching at Catholic

University. He visited both families, but the old easy relationship with Fitzgerald was spoiled by the writer's pathological drinking and erratic behavior, for Barron was afraid of his occasional vindictive reactions. Barron continued to think, however, that Fitzgerald's early training would lead him back to the Church, and he kept track of him until Fitzgerald's death. A decade later, in spite of Barron's interest and prediction, Fitzgerald died outside the Church and was denied her final comfort.

Their patience with life in provincial St. Paul quickly dissipated, and in October 1922 the Fitzgeralds returned to the East, to Great Neck on Long Island. There they lived for a year and a half in the sort of extravagance that the hero of his next novel raised to an art. Although Fitzgerald enjoyed the revels and luxury, the moralist in him was beginning to sense his deterioration and the malaise that he would record in the confessional "Crack-Up" articles a decade later. The pattern of escape was repeated when the Fitzgeralds went to Europe in May 1924, this time for an extended stay. After a summer of hard work on the Riviera, the Fitzgeralds spent the winter in Rome, where he worked assiduously on the galleys of *The Great Gatsby,* which was published in April 1925. Exhausted by the fortunate concentration and extraordinary discipline which are evident in this, his finest work, Fitzgerald returned in the summer to the South of France, the opening scene of his next novel. Here was set into motion the debacle that would end with Zelda's breakdown, the collapse of their marriage, and Fitzgerald's own crack-up.

"Absolution"

Fitzgerald's short stories often illuminate his novels. Just as several of his juvenile pieces finally were incorporated in the pastiche of his first novel, so two of his finest stories are closely related to his third and most artistically successful novel. Fitzgerald discarded the first chapter of *The Great Gatsby,* which described Jay Gatsby's early life, reworked it as a short story, named it "Absolution," and published it in Mencken's *Smart Set* and *American Mercury* and in his 1926 volume *All the Sad Young Men.*

With "Winter Dreams," also included in *All the Sad Young Men*, "Absolution" fleshes out the mysterious past of Fitzgerald's shadowy, mythic hero. While "Winter Dreams" concerns the yearning of Fitzgerald's young man after the Golden Girl, the wealth which is the requisite to having her, and the destructiveness of time, "Absolution" explicates Gatsby's early religious training and his boyhood spiritual crisis which profoundly affects the nature of his mature dream. It is not surprising that Gatsby shares with Basil, Amory Blaine, and Fitzgerald a midwestern Catholic background.

In letters written in 1924 and a decade later, Fitzgerald established the thematic relationship of "Absolution" to *The Great Gatsby*.[19] Furthermore, the publishing and critical history of "Absolution" establishes its artistic kinship with the novel. Both works were part of that confused time in Fitzgerald's life when he was alternately leading a prodigal and ascetic life, when he was turning out glib articles and his formula stories for the popular magazines and writing fiction of the quality of *The Great Gatsby*. And just as *The Great Gatsby* was an artistic success but a financial failure, so "Absolution" was rejected by all of the glossy magazines, and while Fitzgerald's potboilers were selling for $2,500, it was finally sold to *Smart Set* and *American Mercury* for $300 and $118, respectively.

"Absolution" was singled out for praise by the contemporary reviewers of *All the Sad Young Men*, and its compressed style and effect were compared favorably with these aspects of *The Great Gatsby*.[20] The importance of its Catholic orientation was noted by Frances Newman, the critic who reviewed it for the *New York Herald Tribune*, who wrote that "it shows an American Catholic boyhood as clearly as James Joyce showed an Irish Catholic boyhood in the earlier chapters of *A Portrait of the Artist as a Young Man*." [21] In more recent Fitzgerald criticism, "Absolution" is consistently mentioned as one of his finest short stories, and its intrinsic relationship to *The Great Gatsby* has been affirmed. Malcolm Cowley cites its nostalgia for Fitzgerald's Catholic boyhood and the fact that even though Fitzgerald excluded it from *The Great Gatsby*, it retains its connection with the novel,[22] while Henry Dan Piper feels that the source of moral judgment in both "Absolution" and *The Great Gatsby* is the faith in which Fitzgerald had been raised and that the story provides a gloss for the religious background of the novel. He suggests that the novel is so much less overtly Catholic than "Absolution" because when Fitzgerald was writing it his feelings about the Church were as chaotic as those of Amory Blaine, and he could not view or use objectively the Catholic elements and attitudes which had been instilled in him.[23] Although the importance of "Absolution," both for its own merit and as a gloss for *The Great Gatsby,* has been established merely by the idea's frequency in the criticism, the real critical job has hitherto been left undone. A close reading of "Absolution" and a systematic working through the correspondences of imagery, style, theme, and moral tone of the story and the novel cogently demonstrate their connection at several levels.

The mythic character Jay Gatsby and the ritualistic tone of his novel are suggested in the language of the opening of "Absolution." [24]

> There was once a priest with cold, watery eyes, who in the still of the night, wept cold tears. He wept because the afternoons were warm and long, and he was unable to attain a complete mystical union with the Lord. (159)

The Apollonian-Dionysian opposition—the antithesis of light and dark, sun and moon, life and death—is reversed here, just as the blessed light in "The Ordeal" and "Benediction" are identified with the essence of evil. (In *The Great Gatsby* the multiple light images of "Absolution," the allure of the carnival lights and the amber caution of the candlelight of Father Schwartz's words, converge in the image of the green light at the end of Daisy's dock which is a symbol of romantic possibility for Gatsby, the siren's signal, and finally Nick's paean to the future.) For the priest there is no escape from the "hot madness" of four o'clock, when the fecundity of the wheat fields he sees from his window is terrible for him to look upon. The crazed priest prays aloud for the twilight to come, to be free of the "terrible dissonance" of the laughter of the golden Swede girls who pass under his window, who are reminiscent of the peasant girl who had lured Chevalier O'Keefe to his death and eternal damnation. On his Saturday night walks back to

the rectory after hearing confessions, titillated by the revelations he
has heard, his consciously unwilling but nonetheless persistent
attraction to the sensual makes him seek out the gleaming yellow
lights and the "desperately sweet" scent of cheap toilet soap
emanating from the drugstore where the young gather for the
mating dance. The violence done to his sensibility by the antithesis
of his nature and the asceticism of the life he has chosen, the
terrible repression he has experienced, are evident in his mad
confusion of the sacred and profane. He walks on the opposite side
of the street "so that the smell of the soap would float upward
before it reached his nostrils as it drifted rather like incense, toward
the summer moon" (159). In his "haunted room" in the midst of
one of his mad reveries, Father Schwartz is interrupted by
Rudolph Miller, a "beautiful, intense" little boy who sits in a
patch of sunshine with his burden of guilt. When the boy tells him
he has sinned, the priest blurts out, "A sin against purity?"
revealing his own obsession. Resolving to forget his own agony and
to try to assume his priestly role, Father Schwartz attends to his
youthful parishioner's confession, wearing the mask of moral
resiliency he is still able instantaneously to create. This early
introduction of the father-confessor, just as Nick Carraway is
introduced first in *The Great Gatsby,* is one of what Perosa calls the
story's "stylistic warnings." [25]

There follows a long flashback section, the boy's narrative of
the events of the last three days. Rudolph's father had insisted that
he go to confession after a month of avoidance of the sacrament,
and Fitzgerald effectively describes Rudolph's sense of sin and his
fear at having to admit his boyish violations of the Sixth and Ninth
Commandments, the black marks of his sexual offenses upon his
soul. His examination of conscience culminates in his mighty
attempt truly to be penitent, not because he is afraid, but because
he has offended God. But he must first convince himself that he is
sorry before he can convince God. Finally he feels that he has
survived another crisis in his religious life and that he is ready to
enter "that large coffin set on end" (161). But just as the novice in
"The Ordeal" had been tempted before a sacramental act, so a
"demoniac notion" partially possesses Rudolph after he has
entered the confessional as he waits for the sinner who occupies the

far side of the box to finish. He will leave and tell his mother one of two lies; that he had been too late and had found the priest gone or that he had indeed gone to Confession. In any event, he must avoid Communion at mass the next day, "for Communion taken upon an uncleansed soul would turn to poison in his mouth, and he would crumple limp and damned from the altar-rail" (161). His nightmare of eternal damnation is punctuated by the priest's opening the latticed slat before him.

The small sins, easy to recite, come first—swearing, slander, disobedience, smoking, refusing to believe that he is the son of his parents, the fantasy of Stephen Palms in "The Romantic Egoist" and Jay Gatsby—the family romance. Only the difficult ones remain, and, deeply ashamed, he forces himself to speak. Rudolph's sins of "dirty words and immodest thoughts and desires" intrigue Father Schwartz, an indication both of his own pathology and the Church's puritanical preoccupation. The girl who had been party to the sin becomes for both the priest and Rudolph the focus of their censure, an attitude congruent with Augustine's and Fitzgerald's view of women and the traditional though tacit attitude of the Church. The girl was, according to Father Schwartz, the occasion of the boy's sin, and she is transmogrified in Rudolph's mind into one of "the dull and hard-eyed incorrigible girls" one finds in "house[s] of delinquency" (163). As an afterthought, Father Schwartz asks Rudolph if he has told any lies, and with this the crisis of his young life is precipitated. He tells the lie which Fitzgerald had told during his time at Miss Nardins Academy in Buffalo and which he recorded in his Ledger. Rudolph confidently replies to the priest's question, "Oh, no, Father, I never tell lies" (163). He instinctively and habitually lies, but he has enormous respect for the truth, and besides, he knows that to lie to God is the most grievous sin of all. He must fix this bad mistake, but before he can confess, the absolution has been given and the lattice is closed.

As he emerges from the church, Rudolph assumes the persona of his noble and heroic alter ego, Blatchford Sarnemington, the counterpart of Fitzgerald's and Stephen Palms's Stuart king, who will later be named Jay Gatsby. This product and personification of Rudolph's romantic imagination and fictive impulse is a guilty

secret for him, for Blatchford Sarnemington occupies the corner of
Rudolph's mind where he is "safe from God, where he prepared
the subterfuges with which he often tricked God" (163). This
fictive faculty and agent invents a scheme whereby Rudolph can
avoid Communion the next day; he will drink water "by accident"
and be unable to receive the Host. However, Rudolph has to
contend with his earthly father, Carl Miller, in some respects a
fictional counterpart of Edward Fitzgerald. The elder Miller had
floated west with a wave of German and Irish stock, but the
weaknesses in his personality, his restlessness, undependability,
grossness, and suspiciousness made him unable to exploit the
possibilities of that time and place. His only true bonds with life
are his Roman Catholic faith and his worship of James J. Hill, who
is the apotheosis of those qualities Miller lacks—vitality and the
capacity for concrete accomplishment. His envious worship of Hill,
his blind adherence to his faith, and his harsh insistence upon his
family's orthodox observance of its laws have made him a figure of
both contempt and fear to his son. Rudolph's romanticism, his
admiration of the Horatio Alger books, and his invention of
Blatchford Sarnemington, which name he repeats like a litany
when he feels compelled to escape the tedium and oppression of his
life, is his legacy from his father, but he has not yet been
embittered by life's vagaries. On the other hand, while there is
some affection between the father and son, Rudolph despises the
mother of this family, an ineffectual neurotic whose nervous
femininity provides no more than a thin, pastel backdrop for the
perpetual warfare of its two male members.

Rudolph's insistence upon the appearance of truth in the
context of a lie makes him leave a wet glass as evidence by the
kitchen sink, but he is caught by his father before he can drink the
water. Rudolph would tell the truth—that to receive the sacrament
in his state would be sacrilege great enough to tempt thunder-
bolts—but he fears his father more than this, not the beating so
much as the savage ferocity behind it, the beating an outlet for this
ineffectual man. In an instant of rebellion, Rudolph dashes the
glass into the sink, and his father attacks him brutally. Just as the
incident of the lie in Confession came out of Fitzgerald's past, so he
drew upon his own experience for the account of this beating.
Edward Fitzgerald had once struck his son, and it was so

anomalous an act that Fitzgerald recorded it in his Ledger. It was, however, a mere ritualistic spanking, provoked by Scott's staying out too late; the savage blows inflicted by Carl Miller, who is not in every particular a representation of Fitzgerald's father, a gentle and retiring man, are another matter. The father of Jay Gatsby, who appears at the end of the novel, is more nearly a portrait of Edward Fitzgerald—weak, still praising James J. Hill, but gentle in his love for his dead son. But there is a vestige of Carl Miller in him, for he recalls his son's rejection of him, Jay's accusation that he "et like a hog" and that he beat him for it.

The injustice of the father, whose blind misplaced convictions have driven the son to hatred for him, is compounded when he attempts to force the boy to confess his disrespect for his parent. Knowing that this man's sin against him has been more grave than his own, he rejects forever compliance with his father's corrupt system of morality. In the confessional before Sunday mass, Rudolph, in language used by a seminarian rather than an eleven-year-old boy, simply accuses himself of missing his morning prayers. For the first time, Rudolph knows the isolation of one who eschews conventions and appearances for the integrity of his inner life. During mass, when the collection basket passes and he has no money to drop in, Rudolph remembers his shame, another important thematic connection between "Absolution" and *The Great Gatsby*, for this acute embarrassment about his financial status is, of course, an essential component of the character of Jay Gatsby. But even though he has rejected his father and seemingly his faith, when the bell signaling Communion is rung, the dread of God revives in Rudolph, and he goes forward to commit his sacrilege to the appropriate intonation,

> *Domine, non sum dignus; ut intres sub tectum meum; sed tantum dic verbo, et sanabitur anima mea.*
> [Lord, I am not worthy that you should enter my house; but only say the word and my soul will be healed.]

With this description of Rudolph's sure knowledge of his utter damnation, the long retrospective section of the story ends, and the mythic tone of the opening returns.

Rudolph was . . . drenched with perspiration and deep in
mortal sin. As he walked back to his pew the sharp taps of his
cloven hoofs were loud upon the floor, and he knew that it was
a dark poison he carried in his heart. (169)

Perhaps Father Schwartz has heard Rudolph's recitation, but
the only thing of which he is aware is "the beautiful little boy with
eyes like blue stones, and lashes that sprayed open from them like
flower-petals" (169). Now driven totally mad by the course his
repressed sexuality has taken, Father Schwartz suffers a hallucina-
tion in which the "beads of his rosary were crawling and squirming
like snakes" on his table, and the only response to Rudolph's story
he can muster is the cryptic statement: "When a lot of people get
together in the best places things go glimmering" (169). His insane
vision of light, glimmering sensuality and conviviality, replaces in
his consciousness the terrible darkness of his guilt and isolation.
The priest describes for Rudolph the amusement park, "a thing
like a fair, only much more glittering" with "a big wheel made of
lights turning in the air" (171), an image meant to suggest a Ferris
wheel. It is probably also an allusion to the vision of Ezekiel, which
prefigured the destruction of the holy city of Jerusalem. The priest
is, in fact, Rudolph's Ezekiel, for in his depraved vision of
blessedness is prefigured Rudolph's fall from grace, his rejection of
God and His City, and his being blinded by the carnival lights of
the secular world he chooses. Father Schwartz tells Rudolph to go
to see the amusement park where everything seems suspended like
a colored balloon, "like a big yellow lantern on a pole" (the light
on Daisy's dock). But he cautions Rudolph to stand off from it in a
dark place; "don't get up close," he warns, "because if you do
you'll only feel the heat and the sweat and the life" (171).

   This vision is Fitzgerald's metaphor for the active secular
world, variously described as an amusement park, carnival, circus,
or the "world's fair," which appears in his notebooks, in all of the
novels, and in several stories.[26] The amusement park Father
Schwartz describes is the earthly paradise, the City of Man, the
"something ineffably gorgeous somewhere that had nothing to do
with God" (171). Rudolph is sure that it exists. In his desire to see
similarities between the Cities of God and Man, not yet able to see
their marked differences, which will become apparent only after

years and heartbreaking experience, Rudolph thinks that God is no longer angry about the lie. He is sure that God understood that he had told it to make things better in the confessional, that he had brightened his dingy admissions with heroic vision. When he had done it, with his prolific fictive impulse he conjures up a picture of silver pennons, the crunch of leather, the shine of silver spurs, and a troop of horsemen poised for battle, a boy's version of Gatsby's dream. Rudolph does not heed the priest's warning of danger in such splendid visions; as Jay Gatsby he will try to create his own amusement park, and, like a squire who has prayed through the night of his childhood, he will assume the role of a knight in pursuit of the grail he imagines Daisy Fay to be.

Rudolph runs from the room where Father Schwartz, now totally broken, mutters "heart-broken words" and cries out to God some inarticulate plea. The story ends with a celebration of sensuality and fecundity, and the sexuality of the Swede girls which Father Schwartz had screened from his consciousness is now apparent. Rudolph, in the full of pulsing sexual consciousness and the new isolation of adolescence looks squarely at "the heat and the sweat and the life" with the imagination of the artist. The City of Man, populated by those who live according to the flesh, not the spirit, will be Rudolph's dwelling place, for he now realizes that Blatchford Sarnemington is not a mask, but the personification of his inner life.

Two fathers have failed Rudolph. His own parent's bitter dream of material wealth and his cruel piety are sources of his contempt. Moreover, Father Schwartz's diseased imagination renders him unable to give Rudolph a vision of the City of God, just the tawdry of the amusement part, which is ultimately inadequate to the needs of the man of imagination with a strong moral sense. It is impossible for Rudolph to attain the vision of Augustine; rather, like Gatsby, the nightmare world of Petronius will be his realm, and he will be its Trimalchio.[27]

The Great Gatsby

At the same time that Zelda was complaining that her husband had started a new novel and had retired into strict seclusion and celibacy, the monk manqué wrote to his editor, Max Perkins, that he had been trying to outline a new novel whose locale would be the Middle West and New York of 1885 and which would have a Catholic element. Two years later, in 1924, when the novel was completed, there had been some changes in the original scheme, but the "Catholic element" remained. *The Great Gatsby* is not an overtly Catholic work like "The Ordeal" or "Benediction," nor does it contain the profusion of Catholic references found in *This Side of Paradise.* It is obviously the product of Fitzgerald's Catholic consciousness, however, insofar as its original prologue establishes that Gatsby's background is a midwestern Catholic boyhood. Moreover, we shall see that the carnival metaphor which is central to the novel is elucidated by Father Schwartz's mad vision and that the moral sense of the novel, which Nick calls "provincial squeamishness," is based upon the Augustinian antitheses of spirit and matter and the contention that allegiance to an earthly vision rather than a heavenly one will pull one down into the heat and sweat of damnation.

The Great Gatsby [28] is the rest of the story of the career of Jay Gatsby which began when, as a boy eager for an anchor for his imagination, he vainly rejected God for the tenets of a materialistic society and was drawn like a moth to the fatal carnival lights. With the innocence and wonder that had made his Catholic indoctrination so effective, Gatsby commits himself to the false values of materialism and adapts the residual symbolism of his faith and ritualistic habit of spirit to his new religion. He becomes a celebrant-priest dedicated to the ritualized acquisition of wealth and the futile pursuit of an idealized City of Man. At the center of his vision of the ideal is Daisy Fay, who is more to him than a particular woman; rather she is the embodiment of the rich life he seeks, and with a religious fervor he worships and pursues her. When Nick first sees Gatsby he is standing on the lawn of his temple, and he is puzzled by Gatsby's stretching out his arms toward the dark water "in a curious way" just as he had five years earlier stretched out his hand desperately to grasp a fragment of the place Daisy had made lovely for him as he leaves Louisville after her marriage, priestly gestures both of longing and benediction. He is keeping a vigil over the votive light at the end of Daisy's dock with the same sacramental reverence he displays when, in his spare cell-like room at the top of his gaudy mansion, he shows Daisy and Nick his shirts. Moreover, in grotesque parody of the divine office, Gatsby celebrates the Sabbath with secular love feasts which glorify the sensual life. On Sunday mornings while church bells ring in the surrounding villages, "the world and its mistress returned to Gatsby's house and twinkled hilariously on his lawn" (61). But Nick's epic list of Gatsby's guests with its sinister annotations undercuts this gaiety with its reminder that the destiny of the revelers is damnation.

Aside from Gatsby with his priestly dedication, two other characters in the novel suggest its intrinsic religious nature. Dr. Eckleburg keeps his vigil over the wasteland, Fitzgerald's metaphor for the desolation of modern life; he is an anti-God in this sterile world of false values. This representation of God as an advertisement points up the sort of distortion of religious values that had taken place in America in the years after World War I, when the association of business with religion was common. Many American churches formed advertising and publicity departments, and men of religion looked to Christ's life for practical examples. Christ was, according to one of them, the most popular dinner guest in Jerusalem and the founder of modern business. Furthermore, it was believed that His apostles were a model executive staff, and His parables were His most powerful advertisements.[29] When George Wilson points to the Eckleburg billboard during his righteous sermon to his wife and says "God knows what you've been doing. . . . You may fool me, but you can't fool God!" (160), he demonstrates that he is a man of his time and place; this incident is also an illustration of the sort of secularization of the American Dream which Fitzgerald decried and treated ironically in this novel. The Greek friend of George Wilson, Michaelis, is the only proponent of religion in the book; he is, in fact, the Archangel Michael in earthly form.[30] In the lore of Catholicism Michael's primary job is to rescue souls from Satan, especially at the time of death, and to lead them from earth to Judgment. Michaelis is the first to reach Myrtle Wilson after she has been hit by Gatsby's car, and then he comforts her husband, who cries "Oh, my God!" repeatedly in his grief. Michaelis tries to persuade Wilson to accept

the help of a priest and is shocked when Wilson refers to Eckleburg
as the eyes of God. However, all of Michaelis's efforts to correct
Wilson's perceptions and to lead him away from his false idol,
Eckleburg, and back to God are fruitless, as they must be in this
godless world.

The focus of the secular world of this novel is the romantic
readiness, the dream of Jay Gatsby; but in this work Fitzgerald is a
critic of the romantic egoism which he had glorified in *This Side of
Paradise*. Experience had taught Fitzgerald that sophomoric egoism
and ostentatious apostasy were less than gratifying to the spirit.
Although he had rejected the sectarian dogma of Catholicism
along with Amory Blaine, he retained for himself and as the
thematic basis of *The Great Gatsby* the moral values of that faith
which call into question the worthiness of Gatsby's dream. *The
Great Gatsby* is, as Piper suggests, "a retreat toward, though by no
means into, the bosom of Mother Church." [31] The seeds of the
secularization of the vision of Gatsby *(ne* Rudolph Miller) were
dormant in him even before his crisis with Father Schwartz. His
father's worship of James J. Hill had apparently influenced the
boy, for Rudolph sleeps among his Alger books, the primers of the
American self-made man and chronicles of the American secular
myth. Gatsby's father brings with him to his son's funeral the copy
of *Hopalong Cassidy* in which the young Jimmy Gatz had outlined
his Franklinesque schedule for material self-improvement, and in
the juxtaposition of these American heroes is seen a rationale for
his life. The largely self-serving, lawless justice of the American
West represented by Cassidy has been Gatsby's approach in his
business dealings, and in his rise through ingenuity from poverty to
affluence he has followed the example of Franklin, in a part of his
life and career the prototypical American materialist. But just as
Franklin and the settlers of the West also served a higher ideal, so
Gatsby with the religious conviction peculiar to saints, pursues an
ideal, a mystical union, not with God, but with the life embodied
in Daisy Fay.

It had been impossible for the young Gatsby with his energy
and guilty imagination to remain within the Church, which is
antipathetic to these impulses, but with his residual religious fervor
and ritualistic habit of mind he moves into the realm of secular

mythology and becomes a hero-priest. As if his brilliance would blind the beholder, a mythic character is difficult to visualize and is inhuman in his dedication to a cause. Fitzgerald himself did not know what Gatsby looked like and, in fact, was apprehensive about what effect his protagonist's vagueness might have upon the reception of the book. Gatsby's person is never described; his past is shadowed in myth; and the other characters endlessly speculate about him. Nick's vision of Gatsby is at first blinded by his affluence and style, but he soon finds himself looking at "an elegant young roughneck" whose formal speech seems absurd to him. However, when Gatsby, using the same fictive impulse and creative passion with which Rudolph Miller created Blatchford Sarnemington, gives Nick his fictitious account of his past and education, for a time Nick believes in the reality of Gatsby's spurious story. According to Gatsby he is the orphaned son of a wealthy midwestern family, and when Nick asks him what part of the Middle West he is from, he replies "San Francisco." Supposedly he had been educated at Oxford and had lived in all the capitals of Europe collecting jewels and hunting big game. He had been decorated by every Allied government for his heroism in the war, and through it all he had been trying to forget some profound and mysterious sadness. After Gatsby's recitation, Nick believes that it is all true, and he can see his palace on the Grand Canal and his chest of rubies. Nick quickly regains his relative objectivity, however, and places Gatsby's tale in the perspective of the unreality and wonder of this carnival world.

In the character of Nick Carraway, Fitzgerald meant to create another Marlow, Conrad's observer and chronicler who tries to bring some order out of the puzzling events he witnesses. But unlike Marlow, Nick is an interesting and rounded character in his own right. Nick and Gatsby respectively embody the two warring strains of their creator's personality. If Gatsby is an expression of the conspicuous consumer, the dreamer and yearner after the Golden Girl and great wealth, the willing participant in the carnival, then Nick is the moralistic, though imperfect, chronicler of the carnival's follies. Nick is the righteous priest, the confessor and censor, who upholds the established order. Nick is saved from the snares of the carnival by his diffidence, while Gatsby rushes headlong to his destruction, his sense of holy mission having negated the early moral orientation he shares with Nick. Nick's innocence is apparent when the luncheon at the Buchanans is interrupted by Myrtle Wilson's call. He does not understand Jordan's explanation that Tom has "got some woman in New York," and when he does finally perceive the situation, he observes that to some it might have seemed intriguing, but his impulse is to call immediately for the police. He adheres to the old religion of his father, a religion of special privilege and complacency, the sort of Catholic orientation Fitzgerald had had as a boy.

Nick decides after his sojourn in the East that his roots are in the Middle West, and that he is "a little complacent from growing up in . . . a city where dwellings are still called through decades by a family's name." (177) This sense of permanency has made Nick unadaptable to life in the East, and it is clear soon after his arrival that his stay will be a brief one. When he looks for lodging on Long Island with a coworker, he finds a "cardboard bungalow," and his housemate and pet dog desert him within a few days. His only companion in this alien place is his housekeeper, who "mutters Finnish wisdom to herself" [8] At the end his memory of the East is a night scene from El Greco. He remembers a hundred grotesque houses, submissive under a sullen sky and dull moon. Into this scene four men in dress suits carry a drunken woman dressed in white, her hand ornamented with cold, sparkling jewels hanging over the side of the litter. The men turn in gravely at the wrong house, for no one knows the woman's name and no one cares. This scene is an emblem of the experience of all the midwesterners in the novel—Nick, Gatsby, and the Buchanans. Both the constructions of this decadent society an a distorted nature form an uncongenial milieu, and the appearances of elegance cannot mask carelessness and indifference to the identity and health of the spirit. The drunken woman in white, an analogue of Daisy and Jordan Baker, is corruption masked by the semblance of innocence whose true nature is signaled by her insensibility and the sterile ornaments of this society's false values which she wears.

However, Nick is also a "spoiled priest," one who can see the shallowness and vanity of the City of Man, who is, as he says, "full of interior rules that act as brakes on [his] desires" (59), but who cannot totally restrain himself from participation, albeit guilty and tenuous participation, in this world. Nick has a brief affair with a coworker which is abruptly ended by her brother, and in his lonely evenings in New York, he watches women on the street and imagines that he is going to enter their lives and, ever concerned with convention and appearances, that no one would know or disapprove. On the other hand, he enters into a relationship with Jordan Baker although he is aware of her insidious nature, and he plays the pander at Gatsby's request. Furthermore, Nick's position as moral arbiter in the world of the novel is weakened by his response to Gatsby's shady business proposition; he turns it dowñ as a matter of etiquette, since it is bad form, according to Nick, for Gatsby to offer payment for a favor. His final posture of reserving judgment, which he says is "a matter of infinite hope" (1), expresses the strong romantic strain in his character, and the scorn he feels for Gatsby is mitigated by his censure of those who preyed upon him. Nick's conventional morality is not enough to compensate for his defective vision. His inability to correct the distortion he has seen in the East, his failure to recognize the futility and criminality of Gatsby's sacrifice for Daisy show him to be as ineffectual a force for good as Dr. Eckleburg, his correlative in the novel. Even relatively good men like Nick fail to achieve a blessed vision unless they seek it beyond the worldly vanity of the City of Man.

The theme of failed paternity is prominent in *The Great Gatsby,* for the moral failure of both Gatsby and Nick is attributable in part to the nature of their respective paternities. Both ill-equipped sons seek fortune and end their quests unsuccessfully, and in the cyclical movement of the novel they return in failure to their fathers. Nick, armed only with his father's smug prescription for tolerance and after much experience as a father-confessor to the secrets of strangers, sets out for the East to learn the bond business. His paternity seems sound since his family are prominent well-to-do people who have been established in their city for three generations. The Carraways have a tradition that they are descended from the Scot dukes of Buccleuch, but the actual founder of the line was Nick's granduncle who sent a substitute to the Civil War and started a wholesale hardware business which is still the family's livelihood. After telling the story of the wicked East and Gatsby's destruction, Nick returns, tired of glimpses into the human heart and wanting "the world to be in uniform and at a sort of moral attention forever" (2). Nick is still seeking a moral absolute in the chimerical City of Man, and like Gatsby he is doomed to failure.

Neither Gatsby's natural or spiritual father has been able to provide him with values or a vision worthy of his spirit. Mr. Gatz is essentially a good man, he is conventionally virtuous, but even though he subscribes to the American formula for success, he has neither the talent nor temperament to make his way. We have seen that the young Gatsby's appeal to a spiritual father merely strengthened his notion that religion offered nothing to nourish him. At seventeen James Gatz forever rejected his natural parents— "his imagination had never really accepted them as his parents at all" (99)—and created the persona Jay Gatsby as he rowed out to Dan Cody's yacht. For over a year Gatz had lived an itinerant existence along the shore of the lake, his heart in a constant turbulent riot, haunted by visions of "ineffable gaudiness," the corruption of the "something ineffably gorgeous somewhere that had nothing to do with God" which Rudolph Miller had been convinced existed for him. In his nightly dreams, the victim of his own romantic readiness, Gatz sees the "promise that the rock of the world was founded securely on a fairy's wing" (100).

When he meets Dan Cody, Jay Gatsby springs full-blown from his platonic conception of himself, "a son of God" fit to "be about his Father's business, the service of a vast, vulgar, and meretricious beauty" (99). But this is a Trimalchio, not a Christ, and the God he worships is Mammon. Gatsby's foster father, Dan Cody, is a self-made millionaire from transactions in Montana copper, a pioneer debauchee who had transported to the East the violence of the frontier brothel and saloon. His name is the amalgam of Daniel Boone, the pioneer, and William Cody, the buffalo slaughterer and charlatan carnival man, which makes him an apt guide through the tawdry carnival which Father Schwartz had cautioned Rudolph to avoid. Cody is, in effect, John the Baptist to this "Son of God," for Cody has been preaching the materialistic word and passes on the mantle to this false messiah who will carry it to his tragic end. During his time with Cody, Gatsby learns not to drink, for the foolish Cody, who was vulnerable when drinking, had been victimized by women as Chevalier O'Keefe had been. An especially bitter lesson for him evolves out of Dan Cody's $25,000 legacy of which he was cheated by Cody's last female companion. He is never to be a man of inherited wealth, so he sets about His Father's business, amassing a fortune by any means. Three fathers had failed Gatsby, and even Nick, who scolds him for his rudeness before his first meeting with Daisy and who acts as his father-confessor, fails to save him.

When Gatsby lies dead amidst the ineffable gaudiness of his earth-bound vision, his natural father arrives from the West to witness his end. Certain ironic parallels between the figures of Christ and Gatsby are unmistakable,[31] and the description of Gatsby's death and burial is a striking example of Fitzgerald's use of elements of the Christian myth in telling the story of his bogus Christ. Gatsby's gratuitous sacrifice for Daisy, like Christ's for mankind, is the direct cause of his violent death; but this travesty of Christ is scourged by his profound disappointment rather than by Roman soldiers as the death scene approaches, for Nick conjectures that Gatsby must have felt a sharp sense of loss and futility for having lived too long with a single dream. Refusing help, Gatsby carries to his pool a pneumatic mattress which will bear the burden of his dead body. At noon George Wilson is seen on Gad's [God's] Hill, and the murder will occur at about three in the afternoon, the hour of Christ's death. Like Christ, Gatsby is left among strangers during a three-day vigil, and "On the third day" (167) his true identity is resurrected with the telegram of Henry C. Gatz of Minnesota. When he arrives to reclaim his son, he reveals the meager quality of his parentage in his pride at Gatsby's affluence, which overwhelms his grief, and in his statement to Nick that if Gatsby had lived, he would have been a great man like James J. Hill. Just as surely as God sent His son to die for a dream, so Henry Gatz, years before, had set into motion his son's destruction. Gatz had been a derelict earthly father; his worship of materialism, the substance of his earthbound dream for his son, is an ironic analogue to God's purpose for his son.

Fitzgerald was concerned about his characterization of Daisy, who embodies the Augustinian view of women; she is uninteresting compared with Myrtle Wilson and Jordan Baker, he felt, and he was especially troubled by the lack of "emotional backbone" in her relationship with Gatsby. He wrote to H. L. Mencken that the great fault in the book is the lack of any concrete evidence of Daisy's attitude toward Gatsby after their reunion. This had been missed, he said, because it had been concealed beneath elaborate layers of prose. The characterization of Daisy is another case of Fitzgerald's squeamishness, his reluctance to consummate or display sexual passion in his work. In Owen Davis's 1926 dramatization of the novel Daisy offers to become Gatsby's mistress, but her offer is rejected. Thus, Arthur Mizener suggests, "Davis answers the question which Fitzgerald could not." [33] We are told that Gatsby and Daisy had been lovers back in Louisville, but he has so idealized the incident—for he feels he is dedicated to the following of a grail—that it seems to have been more a sacramental than a sensual act. In Gatsby's reminiscence of the night when he took Daisy "because he had no real right to touch her hand" (149), the event is transformed into a mystical experience. In the instant before kissing her, when she becomes the incarnation of his dream, Gatsby's imagination soars to a secret place somewhere above the trees where it romps like the mind of God. He listens for a moment to the music of the spheres and then "forever wed[s] his unutterable visions to her perishable breath" (112).

Gatsby is another of Fitzgerald's frustrated heroes who is incredibly naive about sex. He restores Daisy to her virginal state in his mind by refusing to believe in the reality of her marriage and child, and this illusion is strengthened by the mask of innocence which Daisy wears. She is one of Fitzgerald's vampires, but her destructiveness goes beyond a momentarily broken heart or wounded pride of her male prey. She dresses in white just as she did back in Louisville, and her eyes are free of desire; she uses her voice as a snare and conceals her heart in her "breathless, thrilling words." The white powder with which she and Jordan cover their bodies is, like the foul dust of the wasteland, a sign of their corruption, for these whited sepulchers are deadly vampires beneath their mannered gentility. Daisy is important in the book only insofar as she functions as a symbol for Gatsby, a commodity made more valuable for having been desired by many other men.

She is the Golden Girl high in a white place, the symbol of the grail
Gatsby is committed to pursue. But this vessel holds a substance
poisonous to love and the spirit. This romantic heroine, sym-
bolically dressed in white, a tight hat of metallic cloth and a cape,
is a reincarnation of Morgan le Fay, who deceived all of her
lovers; [34] she is literally the *femme fatale* for Gatsby.

One of the most important correspondences between "Absolution" and *The Great Gatsby* is the prominence of carnival imagery in
the novel, for Rudolph as Gatsby sets out to create his own
amusement park against, as it were, the advice of Father Schwartz.
It becomes clear, however, that it is not just his immediate creation
but all of the City of Man which is a great World's Fair, tawdry
and meretricious in its concept of beauty and corrupt in its sense of
justice. The carnival theme is established immediately with the
poem on the title page which declares that Gatsby will be Daisy's
jester.

> Then wear the gold hat, if that will move her;
> If you can bounce high, bounce for her too,
> Till she cry "Lover, gold-hatted, high-bouncing lover,
> I must have you!"

The milieu of the novel is at first a child's world in which Tom
Buchanan innocuously plays with his horses; Jordan Baker plays
the game of golf; and Daisy, seemingly the helpless innocent, plays
with her doll-child. Gatsby's house is something out of a child's
dream of the residence of an American prince. The automobile is a
peculiarly American symbol of identity, and the cars in the two
playgrounds in this novel, the Eggs and New York, are fantastic
carnival wagons. In New York Myrtle selects a new lavender-
colored car with gray upholstery from the train of taxicabs lined
up at the railroad station. The description of Gatsby's car, which
Tom calls a "circus wagon," is an emblem of his dedication to a
meretricious standard of beauty. After it is clear that this carnival
world is, on the underside of its swollen and monstrous sort of
glamour, a nightmare world, Gatsby's vehicle becomes a "death
car" for him as well as for Myrtle Wilson. This violence is

foreshadowed by Tom Buchanan's auto accident, the incident at the conclusion of Gatsby's party, and the "rotten driver," Jordan Baker, who hates careless people yet depends upon others to avoid accidents. Between the Eggs and New York lies the nameless wasteland of desolate ash heaps where the Wilsons live and the inanimate Dr. Eckleburg watches all that occurs with godly detachment. In Wilson's garage, crouched in a dim corner, is "the dust-covered wreck of a Ford" (25), which bears the name of the godlike creator of the age of the automobile. Here Myrtle Wilson's life is violently extinguished as her blood is mingled with the foul dust that "floated in the wake" of Gatsby's dreams. This valley of ashes is, in contrast to the lush greenery of the Buchanan house and the *nouveau* green of Gatsby's mansion, "a fantastic farm" where, perversely, ashes grow like wheat and grotesque gardens, ironic analogues to the fecund wheat fields Father Schwartz finds horrible to look upon. This place represents the actual nature of the City of Man, and in contrast to this recurrent view of the essential sterility of modern life Fitzgerald shows us the glamorous World's Fair. However, just as Amory Blaine is shown the horrible underside of the carnival, so in this novel Fitzgerald relentlessly reveals its sham, baseness, violence, and the problem of fixing one's identity in a world destitute of spiritual values.

During Nick's trip to New York with Tom and Myrtle, when he is struck by the strangeness of the pastoral scene of Fifth Avenue on a Sunday afternoon, he encounters a crooked pitchman selling dogs, a purveyor of illusion who looks remarkably like John D. Rockefeller. In the apartment cluttered with oversized furniture, to move about is to stumble over scenes of ladies swinging in the gardens of Versailles, the mirrored pleasure dome. As the party becomes chaotic, Nick's perception of the reality beneath the facade of gaiety and conviviality sharpens, and he becomes "simultaneously enchanted and repelled by the inexhaustible variety of life" (36); he is the spoiled priest at the fair. Myrtle's sister, Catherine, attempts to cover her face with a new one, and she appears in clown makeup. Her powdered white complexion is topped with a solid, sticky red bob, and she has plucked her eyebrows and painted on a new pair at a new, more rakish angle. Myrtle's laughter and gestures become violently affected, and as she expands the room seems to grow smaller "until she seemed to be revolving on a noisy, creaking pivot through smoky air" (31) as she is transformed into the laughing lady, a carnival figure of hysterical gaiety.

Among the guests at the party is the photographer, McKee, whose wife tells Nick that he has photographed her a hundred and twenty-seven times since their marriage, apparently in a futile attempt to fix her identity. He is also responsible for the picture of Myrtle's mother, which Nick at first assumes is a hen sitting on a blurred rock. The tempo of the search for identity accelerates as "people disappeared, reappeared, made plans to go somewhere, and then lost each other, searched for each other, found each other a few feet away" (37). Daisy and Jordan are also attractions in this carnival world. When Nick first sees them, they are lying on a couch in the Buchanan circus tent of a living room. The curtains blow "like pale flags," and the women are "buoyed up as though upon an anchored balloon." Their dresses ripple and flutter as though they "had just been blown back in after a short flight around the house," and Jordan performs like a trained seal "with her chin raised a little, as if she were balancing something on it" (8).

With the inventiveness and skill of a Belasco, Gatsby plays the role of Trimalchio in his creation of a carnival world. He plans excursions to Coney Island, and on weekends his Rolls-Royce becomes an omnibus to transport groups of revelers from New York to his home which, according to Nick, resembles the World's Fair. On Mondays a troop of servants with mops, hammers, and garden shears work to repair the ravages of two days of excess, waste, and destruction. Each week five crates of oranges and lemons are turned into a pyramid of pulpless halves, and once a fortnight caterers arrive with several hundred feet of canvas "and enough lights to make a Christmas tree of Gatsby's enormous garden" (39). In a scene reminiscent of Trimalchio's fantastic banquets, "on buffet tables, garnished with glistening hors d'oeuvre, spiced baked hams crowded against salads of harlequin designs and pastry pigs and turkeys bewitched to a dark gold" (39-40). In halls and saloons and verandas gaudy with primary colors, faces and voices and colors are transformed in sea-changes under the constantly changing light as people wander aimlessly in this mercurial sea of pleasure. People are not invited to Gatsby's house; they just come with a "simplicity of heart" that is its own ticket of admission to do "stunts" all over the garden and to conduct themselves "according to the rules of behavior associated with an amusement park" (41).

The garishness of the carnival is also suggested in the account of Gatsby's meeting with Daisy and their tour of his house. The color gold is prominent; the flowers in the garden emit a "pale gold odor"; the brass buttons on Daisy's dress gleam; and there is a pure gold toilet set on Gatsby's dresser which gleams so brightly, when Daisy uses it, that Gatsby must shade his eyes. Gatsby wears a gold tie, and the house itself catches the gold light of the sun. In a climactic act of gaucherie, which is also a sacramental act performed by this celebrant-priest of materialism, Gatsby throws before Daisy and Nick his gaudy wardrobe of shirts. Light is the central image in this carnival as it is in Father Schwartz's mad vision, and the light at the end of Daisy's dock has been the beacon of Gatsby's dream. Now that the siren it represents is within his reach, he seems to regret the loss of the blessed symbol. The significance of the light has vanished forever. It had borne the relationship for him of a star and the moon in its closeness to her, but now it was merely a green light on a dock, and "His count of enchanted objects had diminished by one" (94). Gatsby is beginning to learn the wisdom in Father Schwartz's warning not to get too close to the carnival's light, but he does not yet know that his temerity will ultimately cost him his life as well as his soul.

At Gatsby's second party, Nick senses a new oppressiveness and harshness in the air; the layers of glamour are gradually being stripped from the carnival, and its true nature surfaces. What had amused him a few weeks before "turned septic on the air now" (107), and instead of innocuously trivial conversations the words of the guests are strident, and altercations abound.

Daisy is appalled by Gatsby's menagerie; Gatsby accedes to her wish that it be destroyed, and the "whole caravansary [falls] in like a card house at the disapproval in her eyes" (114). The lights of the carnival go out, and "his career as Trimalchio was over" (113). The mood of the novel changes at this point, and heat and sweat become the predominant images as Fitzgerald cumulatively creates a vision of hell. The immediate events leading to Gatsby's destruction are set into motion on the day of Daisy's luncheon, the hottest day of the year, and on the train Nick notices that the straw seats are near combustion. The woman next to him perspires delicately for a time, but she abruptly lapses into despair with a desolate cry. The conductor chants the word "Hot!" and Nick, associating heat and sexuality, wonders "whose flushed lips he kissed, whose head made damp the pajama pocket over his heart" (115). When Nick and Gatsby arrive at the Buchanans' house, Nick's perceptions rendered surrealistic by the heat, he imagines that the butler shouts into the phone, "The master's body? . . . I'm sorry, madame, but we can't furnish it—it's far too hot to touch this noon!" (115), a foreshadowing of Gatsby's death and an allusion to the Eucharist and the Last Supper. When the party drives in the oppressive heat to New York, Tom stops at Wilson's garage for gasoline, and there he learns that Wilson plans to take Myrtle away. Enraged by the knowledge that he has lost his wife and mistress in one day, Tom drives off feeling "the hot whips of panic" toward New York, which had been described by Nick as a heavenly city of endless exciting possibilities. It is now a sensuous Eden, "overripe, as if all sorts of funny fruits were going to fall into your hands" (125). In the hotel suite, where it is revealed to Gatsby that his dream had been founded on nothing more secure than a fairy's wing, the heat is stifling, but after Daisy's betrayal has been accomplished, the party, in separate cars, drives toward death through the cool dying of the day, the holocaust to be consummated later with Gatsby's death.

After the killing of Myrtle Wilson, who lies in the dust giving up her tremendous vitality, her shirtwaist still damp with perspiration, water imagery becomes predominant. Myrtle's sister is driven away "in the wake of her . . . body" while "a changing crowd lapped up against the front of the garage" (156). The next day there is an autumnal flavor in the air, for the season of Gatsby's death has come. He is shot by Wilson as he floats in his pool, the foul dust washed away by the cleansing water as a thin red circle is traced around the body. The postlude recounting the circumstances of Gatsby's burial illustrates the cyclical course of the book suggested in this image. A thick drizzle falls upon Gatsby's grave, and in death he receives the absolution he had sought as a boy, for he had been damned to this inevitability when he had run from the priest's study to pursue a chimerical earthly vision of grace. Nick reflects that Gatsby's "dream must have seemed so close that he could hardly fail to grasp it, [that] he did not know that it was already behind him, somewhere back in that vast obscurity beyond the city [City of Man]" (182).

4.

The Lost Decade: 1924-1934

Fitzgerald received the best critical notices of his career for *The Great Gatsby*, but a critical success does not necessarily sell well, and such was the case with this novel, which sold only 22,000 copies in its first year and barely cancelled Fitzgerald's debt to Scribner's. Before its publication Fitzgerald said that its fate would determine his own. If it were successful, he would continue his career as a serious novelist, and if not he would go to Hollywood to learn the picture business and concentrate his efforts in building popular and economic success. Fitzgerald was never so calculating, however, and he would not so easily forget his keen disappointment at *The Great Gatsby*'s financial failure. For a time he and Zelda sought lethe in "1000 parties and no work," and thus began the difficult and complex ten-year period during which—after it had gone through seventeen stages of three major conceptions—*Tender Is the Night* was written.

These years, which the Fitzgeralds spent alternately in Europe and America, were marked by tragic problems for both of them. Fitzgerald's drinking problem became acute as Zelda's mental deterioration began with her obsessive interest in dancing and was culminated in 1930 in Paris, when she collapsed and her illness was diagnosed as schizophrenia. She would spend the rest of her life as an invalid in and out of institutions. On the Riviera in the summer of 1926, the Fitzgeralds were tolerated rather than welcomed at social gatherings, and in fact were barred from some homes and public places because of their destructive behavior. The antics that had seemed so charming years before when they were the darlings of the Jazz Age now soured along with their dreams of happiness together and great financial and literary success. Through it all, notwithstanding her ultimate breakdown, Zelda was probably the more stable of the two, and she saw at least as clearly as Fitzgerald the dangerous turn their life had taken. She was frightened by his drinking and the distance between them, and she wrote to Max Perkins at the end of the summer of 1926, in language that could have come from one of her husband's novels, "Now all the gay decorative people have left taking with them the sense of carnival and impending disaster that colored the summer." [1]

One of the most striking manifestations of Zelda's disturbance and her resentment of her husband involved her growing absorption in Catholicism which had begun a few years before her breakdown. An obsessive interest in religion is a common symptom of schizophrenia, and eventually this would be true of Zelda as her condition worsened, but at first it was merely a part of her ambivalent feelings for her husband. She went to mass in Paris, perhaps to understand better Fitzgerald's past and the short-lived Catholic experience of their daughter, but Catholicism was also involved in her bitterness toward her husband. The Fitzgeralds were with friends once when, a look of revulsion on her face, Zelda made the apparently irrelevant remark: "I wish I had been born a Catholic." [2] Whether disgust or a feeling of exclusion was behind her expression is not clear, but apparently his Catholicism was an issue between them. Later when she was at Highland Hospital in Asheville, probably partially in the schizophrenic's usual attempt to imitate and please his authority figure, Zelda studied Catholicism and considered converting to her husband's religion. Fitzgerald reacted to this with impatient anger, and he spoke to his daughter of her mother as one of those who are "mere guests on earth, eternal strangers carrying around broken decalogues they cannot read."[3]

Those who knew Fitzgerald in these years have noted the depth of his Catholic consciousness, even at this point in his life. Morley Callaghan reports that Fitzgerald refused to go into St.

Sulpice Cathedral with him because, Fitzgerald said, of "the Irish Catholic background and all that," a reaction which, Callaghan thought, revealed some deep religious sentiment.[4] And Hemingway claimed that it was Fitzgerald's "strange mixed-up Irish Catholic monogamy" which made him remain faithful to his wife and that it was not until she "went officially crazy" that he slept with another woman.[5] Yet Fitzgerald spoke contemptuously of "the candles my mother keeps constantly burning to bring me back to Holy Church,"[6] and he spoke irreverently of the Church in letters to friends from whom he had always tended to hide his Catholicism. To Edmund Wilson he wrote:

> Please don't say you can't come the 25th but would like to come the 29th. It is the anniversary of the 2nd Council of Nicea when our Blessed Lord, our Blessed Lord, our Blessed Lord—It always gets stuck in that place.[7]

And to Ernest Hemingway:

> My temporary bitternesses toward people have all been ended by what Freud called an inferiority complex and Christ called "Let him without sin"—[8]

This was not a productive time for Fitzgerald; he wrote several potboilers and a few isolated good pieces, among them the Basil stories which were his way of exploring the reasons for his condition, and "Babylon Revisited,"[9] in which Paris is the correlative of the City of Man. This story, written after Zelda's first breakdown, is a reflection of Fitzgerald's guilt about the cost to his marriage and child exacted by his and Zelda's dissipation, and his fears at what might happen if he continued in his self-destructive life. He told Harold Ober that this story was founded on a real quarrel with his sister-in-law; in fact, he sent a typescript to Zelda's sister, Rosalind, and told her that it had been inspired by her suggestion that Scottie should live with her.[10] In this story Charlie Wales returns to Paris after an absence of over a year to reclaim his daughter, who is living with his dead wife's sister and her husband. He finds that the big party is over now, that the city—which had been the scene of the dissipation that had brought about his wife's death, his own breakdown, and the loss of his child, seen through his now sober eyes—is not at all appealing. The old time when they had been a sort of infallible, magical royalty and the time later when the expenditure of great sums of money had been "an offering to destiny" seem distant and unreal. Perhaps he is no longer in hell, but this place with "fire-red, gas-blue, ghost-green signs [shining] smokily through the tranquil rain" (386), where "the two great mouths of the Café of Hell still yawned" (389), is his purgatory.

Redemption is now possible for him, for Wales is ready to face the consequences of his folly and to salvage what he can of the past by re-creating a new life with his daughter. Back in the madness of those days when in the intensity of their love they had begun to abase and tear it into shreds, on a particularly irresponsible night, Wales had inadvertently locked his wife out in a snowstorm after a quarrel. During his wife's subsequent illness, Wales was recovering from a breakdown in a sanitarium, and to make her dying easier he agreed to allow her sister to take custody of their daughter. Now he has rebuilt his fortune, and he has stopped drinking except for one cocktail a day which he takes so that alcohol should not become a compelling thing again. He avoids the old friends who were part of the past he must now forget, and he goes to his daughter's foster parents assuming the "chastened attitude of the reformed sinner" (393) to win their confidence and their permission to take his child. Honoria is nine years old, Scottie's age when this story was written, and Wales is as concerned for her patrimony as Fitzgerald was for his daughter's; he hopes that she does not have the traits which brought her parents to disaster.

Wales thinks that the best thing to do for her is to return to a belief in character, the eternally valuable element of his father's generation, for it had worn out in his own. In the past Wales had been strict with the child, but now he extends himself to her not to close any part of her to communication; now before she is utterly crystallized he wants to put something of himself into her. But it would be best, he thinks, not to love too much, for he knows well the damage parents can do by holding their children too closely. The intrusion of some drunken friends ruins Wales's chance to recover his daughter, but he will try again another time when perhaps he can convince his sister-in-law that he is capable of providing a stable existence for the child. This story and the letters he wrote to Scottie after he left her in the care of the Obers and when she was away at eastern schools constitute the most revealing statement we have of Fitzgerald's feelings about his own parenthood.

The old Catholic habits and responses in Fitzgerald would not die. He and Scottie had moved into a house ironically called La Paix on the Bayard Turnbull estate outside Baltimore in the spring of 1932, and there he worked hard to shape the final version of *Tender Is the Night*. Here he found some respite from his torturous work in the Turnbull children, his own daughter, and the Turnbulls' Irish Catholic gardener. Unlike Fitzgerald, the gardener had never been disturbed by intellectuality, and Fitzgerald envied the man's peace. When the gardener's wife died, he went to the quiet wake at their cottage and knelt in prayer beside the coffin. It was a simple gesture from his past, a moment of quiet communion with "someone who could have helped ... to keep his shop open." [11] The despair which Fitzgerald felt when he wrote this phrase in one of the "Crack-Up" articles became a frequent condition in this, the last decade of his life. It was obvious that his wife was incurably ill, and, the vogue of his writing having passed, he found it increasingly difficult to sell his work. But his work was his salvation then as it had always been. That he acknowledged the source of his strength is evident in a document he was asked to write by Zelda's therapist at Phipps in which he said: "As a first premise you have to develop a conscience and if on top of that you have talent so much the better. But if you have talent without the conscience, you are just one of thousands [sic] journalists." [12]

Fitzgerald's already heavy drinking increased during this time, and he began to be bothered by insomnia. He wrote an *Esquire* article on the subject, "Sleeping and Waking," [13] which anticipates the material and tone of the 1936 "Crack-Up" articles he wrote for the same magazine. It begins as a whimsical piece on the pests, mice and mosquitoes, which sometimes plague one in the night, but the more serious comment to come is signaled by this passage.

There is, if one is lucky, the "first sweet sleep of night" and the last deep sleep of morning, but between the two appears a sinister, ever widening interval. This is the time of which it is written in the Psalms: *Scuto circumdabit te veritas eius: non timebis a timore nocturno, a sagitta volante in die, a negotio perambutante in tenebris.* (63) [His faith is a shield and buckler,/ You will not fear the terror of the night, nor the arrow that flies by day, nor the pestilence that stalks in darkness.]

Fitzgerald was never a Latin scholar; he spent his time in Latin class at the Newman School in scribbling at the back of his Latin book, and those few Latin phrases in his work are not classical Latin, but church Latin. This passage is from Psalm 90 in the Latin Vulgate Bible (Psalm 91 in the Revised Standard Version), and it is part of the priest's daily office in the Latin Breviary. The use of this verse, classic words of God's watchfulness over and protection of tortured souls, is certainly congruent with Fitzgerald's, the priest manqué's, lingering Catholic habit of mind. The tone of the article soon passes from whimsy to terror as Fitzgerald describes his nightly bedtime ritual; the water and Luminal close at hand, the changes of pajamas necessitated by his frequently awaking in rivulets of sweat when he squarely faced his mortality. After a brief period of sleep, the waking time of self-recrimination comes when all of the error of his life returns to haunt him, and then it occurs to him that hell must be something like this tortured stasis.

. . . what if this night prefigured the night after death . . . an eternal quivering on the edge of an abyss, with everything base and vicious in oneself urging one forward and the baseness and viciousness of the world just ahead. No choice, no road, no hope—only the endless repetition of the sordid and semi-tragic. (67)

Fitzgerald's Catholic conscience surfaced in these most naked and solitary hours of the night and made him pay for the extravagance and waste of his life. Fitzgerald was harder on himself than his harshest critics, as a man with his sensibility and Catholic orientation had to be.

An incident which occurred in the summer of 1933 involving Charles Warren, a young writer who worked with Fitzgerald on a screen treatment of *Tender Is the Night,* also points up Fitzgerald's lingering Catholic habit of mind. Fitzgerald roused Warren in the middle of the night and somehow found a cooperative Episcopal priest, about whose mood and motives one can only speculate, and Warren was baptized with Fitzgerald standing as his godfather. Even though he had been drinking heavily, still Fitzgerald read all of the responses soberly.[14] This friendship was a short-lived one; however, for a time Fitzgerald assumed a paternal role with Warren, as several priests had with him, and it is telling that he chose to formalize their relationship in a sacrament of the Church.

Fitzgerald was later to tell Sheilah Graham: "the Jesuit priests would say 'Give me a boy until he is seven. By then his character will be formed. Nothing afterwards could much change him.' "[15] Fitzgerald was living evidence of this truism. Reflecting on his career, he wrote to his daughter:

> Sometimes I wish I had gone along with that gang [Cole Porter and Rodgers and Hart], but I guess I am too much a moralist at heart and really want to preach at people in some acceptable form rather than to entertain them.[16]

Preach he did, not only in his letters to Scottie and to her young friend Andrew Turnbull, whom he told to "examine [his] conscience and see if [he had] violated some primary laws ... laid down for [him]," [17] but also in all of his best work, including *Tender Is the Night,* which he called a "confession of faith." [18]

Through this period of hopelessness, by some effort born of his stubborn conscience and belief in his obligation to his own talent, the only belief he had left, Fitzgerald struggled to complete the book for publication. *Tender Is the Night,* Fitzgerald's witness of his emotional and spiritual bankruptcy, was published on April 12, 1934.

Tender Is the Night

Tender Is the Night [19] is Fitzgerald's ultimate delineation of the horrors of the City of Man. Although it might seem to be as distant from the Catholic frame of reference of *This Side of Paradise* [19] and other early works as Fitzgerald was from his Catholic background at this time, beneath the trappings of this product of his secular imagination is Fitzgerald's persistent moralism. This book, like Fitzgerald's other novels, is not a "Catholic novel" in the manner of Graham Greene's books. Dick Diver is not a Catholic—although his wife is—and the specifically Catholic references are fewer and more veiled here than in some of the early writing. But an underlying moral seriousness, Dick's priestly role, and the carnival imagery—perhaps all products of Fitzgerald's Catholic orientation—are important elements of the book.

Dick's priestly role is first played out with Nicole's father; and Dick shares Nicole's ambivalence toward him, for he, too, vaguely feels guilty of incest in his relationship with Nicole. When he goes to Devereux Warren's deathbed to decide if Nicole should be called as Warren had requested, he is a reluctant priest ministering to a sinner with whom he feels complicity. Warren, a Catholic, had been in a religious mood since the beginning of his illness, and now his conscience plays back to him "the coarse melodies of old sins" (248). He is attended by a nun, and he clasps a rosary in his emaciated fingers. He talks with Dick about the religious understanding which has come to him at the end of his life and of the evil he has done, and he tells Dick that "a Bigger Man than either of them" (248) wants Dick to absolve him of his sins and to allow him one more glimpse of Nicole. Dick decides against the meeting, but Nicole learns of her father's imminent death, and by the time she arrives, Warren has disappeared. Apparently strengthened by what he took to be Dick's absolution and probably afraid, as Dick notes, to face in Nicole the evidence of his great sin and his final Judgment, Warren "took up his bed and walked!" (251). Dick attempts to explain this to himself and to Nicole in scientific terms, but he is actually shaken by the "miracle" he has performed.

Like Warren, another important failed parent in the novel is Dick Diver's father, who, for all of his formal goodness and love for his son, has not equipped Dick to meet the demands of the world he enters. Like all of Fitzgerald's fictional sons, Dick has rejected the life-style of his father, though in a sense he follows his father's vocation. The elder Diver is a retired minister; and in his career as a psychiatrist, Dick, too, has been a physician to the soul, though his flock is an expecially unworthy one of rich, spoiled, and irresponsible idlers. In his General Plan for *Tender Is the Night*, Fitzgerald said that the novel should show a man who is a natural idealist, a spoiled priest, one who has fallen from the state of grace but who can never forget what that state was like, a man divided within himself between a heightened purpose and a sense of duty and a deliberate rejection of discipline, a man who gives himself over to excess with the fervor the priest devotes to his office. When Dick realizes the folly of his decision to reject the moral virtues of his father's vocation and to subscribe to the superficial values of taste and charm, he repeatedly refers in his mind to his boyhood state of grace with his father in Buffalo. He attempts to escape in an Alpine holiday from the madness of life with Nicole after she had attempted to kill both of them and their children.

To recover the peace of long ago, Dick goes back in his imagination to his boyhood. From the train window he watches the villages, each one gathered around a church, and in his mind he sits in these churches as he sat in his father's Buffalo church; he is "Crucified, Died, and is Buried" (195). He once more worries about his offering for the collection plate because of the girl who sat in the pew behind. His image of himself as the Son of God is tainted by a significant memory of his boyhood, for he, like Fitzgerald and Rudolph Miller, had been painfully embarrassed by his poverty. Now "wolf-like under his sheep's clothing," a hypocritical lecher, his eyes move from the churches to a peasant girl whose face reminds him of the colors of an illuminated missal, and she, like the Swede girls who tempt Father Schwartz and the peasant girl who draws Chevalier O'Keefe to his damnation, becomes the center of his profane vision.

Even though part of Dick's mind is composed of the tawdry souvenirs of his boyhood, somehow he has managed to keep alive the painful fire of his intelligence, and his "old asceticism" restrains his lust for the girl. In his musing Dick now realizes the full tragic significance of his embarrassment over the collection plate and the girl and the circle of hell where he now finds himself because of his choice of materialistic values. His obsessive resolve to acquire wealth, in spite of his essentially unacquisitive nature, began when he watched his father's struggles in poor parishes. He had never meant to allow himself to be unmanned, swallowed up like a gigolo, but somehow he has permitted himself to be locked up in the Warren safety-deposit boxes.

Dick's heritage has not made him a totally unwitting prey of the corrupt Warrens; rather, like Fitzgerald's other heroes, he is a willing victim of the vicious female destroyers and of the corruption of wealth. His damnation was set into motion, long before he met Nicole, in his moment of embarrassment in his father's church when he freely chose to give his allegiance to the City of Man. In *This Side of Paradise* and *The Great Gatsby,* both a natural father and a priestly father, and thus the Church, fail their sons. In this novel the father and priest are one, and as surely as Amory Blaine and Jay Gatsby found the faith of their fathers uncongenial, so Dick Diver is damned by his father's failure to arm him to meet the world, by the Church's failure to offer him an attractive alternative to materialism, and by his own inability to see that the sublimity of the City of God cannot be destroyed by any earthly institution. Of course, the dilemma of the spoiled priest, the essentially spiritual and good man who is nevertheless possessed of a vital secular imagination, is at the center of Fitzgerald's life and work. This dilemma supplies the ambiguity and tension of *Tender Is the Night,* in which the pain of this situation is more fully drawn and effectively represented than in any of the other novels.

The second person to whom Dick relates as a priest is Nicole, for he is not only in love with her but also is consecrated to completing her cure. She has been traumatized by her incestuous experience with her father when Dick meets her, and in the course of their unorthodox relationship, she transfers her feelings for her father to Dick, who ministers to her. In her desperate need for him to intercede for her, "Nicole brings everything to his feet, gifts of sacrificial ambrosia, of worshipping myrtle" (137). But later, when she is strong and no longer needs Dick's priestly office, Nicole becomes the celebrant of her own vitality and beauty. As she prepares to meet her lover, Tommy Barban, Nicole bathes and anoints herself and covers her body with a layer of powder, a sign (as it is for Daisy and Jordan Baker) of her unscrupulousness, and "crosses herself reverently with Chanel Sixteen" (291).

In his relationship with "Daddy's Little Girl," Rosemary Hoyt, Dick also acts as a father-priest, as he had in the past with a circus clown, a comedienne from the Grand Guignol, and a half-crazy pederast from the Russian Ballet. When at first Dick rejects her, she touches him, "feeling the smooth cloak of his dark coat like a chasuble" (38), and seems about to fall to her knees. Dick waits outside her studio, "his collar molded plastically to his neck" (91), suggesting a Roman collar, "just as another man once found it necessary to stand in front of a church in Ferrara, in sack cloth and ashes [atoning for] things unforgotten, unshriven, unexpurgated" (91). The street Dick stands on is ironically named the "Rue de Saintes Anges" and its shop signs, "Déclaration de Decès," "Vêtements Ecclésiastiques," "Pompes Funèbres," fittingly have to do with both the Church and death, for Dick's willful rejection of his youthful morality is another step to his damnation.

Dick acts as an ineffectual or corrupt priest with several other characters, among them the Iron Maiden, one of his patients who suffers a torturous death, imprisoned in the shell of eczema which covers her body. Dick sits with her through many nights trying to comfort her as she obliquely confesses her life's sins, and he can utter only platitudes which disgust him; even so, they are the only words priests often have to offer: "We must all try to be good" (185). Dick is also the judgmental priest with Mary North Minghetti and Lady Caroline, who dress as sailors and take two local girls to a lodging house on a lark. Called to the jail to extricate them from their difficulty, he nods gravely, "looking at the stone floor, like a priest in the confessional" (304), and he is torn by the dual impulse to laugh with them ironically and to order fifty lashes and a fortnight of bread and water. But it is not as a priest that he helps them; rather he calls upon his charm to free them and to placate the incensed parents of the girls. Dick is a decidedly ineffectual priest; he ultimately teaches no valuable lesson except by his negative example, nor does he comfort anyone.

Fitzgerald called one of the early versions of *Tender Is the Night* "The World's Fair," and it would have been a fitting title had he retained it, for carnival imagery pervades this novel. Immediately Fitzgerald establishes an antithesis between the carnival's gaiety and its sinister underside. The Carnival by the Sea which the Divers create on the Riviera, where flowers seem to be transparent artifices, where the old villa that now houses Gausse's Hotel is rotting like water lilies, is an overripe Eden. Dick is a godlike ringmaster who performs entertainments for his appreciative audience grouped under their multicolored umbrellas. But the images of heat and sweat recalling Father Schwartz's warning to Rudolph Miller soon intrude. Rosemary is so involved in the Divers and their circle that she forgets her virginal white skin and develops a painful sunburn, and later she awakens on the beach bathed in sweat as Dick approaches her. Though she is at first entranced by the beautiful people, listening to the melancholy tunes of the orchestra, which are reminiscent of the music played for vaudeville acrobats, Rosemary soon sees that in spite of the attempts of impresarios like Dick to create gaiety, life in this country is empty and stale. Now even the world Rosemary knows best, the movie studio, is a Dantesque scene; as she moves through the lot at Monte Carlo, she sees ashen faces turned up to her "like souls in purgatory watching the passage of a mortal through" (23).

Shortly after meeting Rosemary, Dick, in what he calls "an apostolic gesture," arranges a party which he hopes will begin in gaiety and then—with a brawl, seductions, and women passing out in the *cabinet de toilette*—turn sour on the air. Beneath his perverse gaiety, Dick is actually the melancholy priest, for when he acknowledges the extravagance and waste of which he is guilty and recalls the "carnivals of affection" he has given, he feels the remorse a general might feel who had ordered a massacre to satisfy his own blood lust. In the same mood he later guides Rosemary across a battlefield of the Great War outside Paris, saddened by the prospect of the place where "all his beautiful lovely safe world blew itself up" (57). Dick's extraordinary virtuosity with people makes all of his guests believe that they are present at a special event, and as they surround the Divers, they seem like "poor children at a Christmas tree" (34). But the holiday mood vanishes as Dick's wish for the party comes true, and the woman in the *cabinet de toilette,* driven mad by her husband's attention to Rosemary, is Nicole. The dizzying ride back to Gausse's Hotel from the Divers' villa is "a series of roller-coaster swoops" (39), and at its end, Rosemary perceives the folly of the Diver carnival.

In Paris, at another party he arranges, Rosemary sees Dick again as the imposing godlike master of the carnival, the "organizer of private gaiety, creator of a richly incrusted happiness" (76). Dick commandeers a fantastic circus wagon for their tour through the city; with its silver wheels and radiator and its interior inlaid with paste jewels it is an emblem of the spurious "richly incrusted happiness" Dick creates. As Dick and Rosemary dance, she feels her beauty sparkling, and he displays her to the crowd as if she were a bright bouquet or a piece of precious cloth, just as Gatsby reverently showed his wardrobe of shirts to Daisy and Nick. The evening ends as Rosemary and the Norths, like children at a fair, ride in a wagon on the top of a load of carrots bound for Les Halles. The underside of the carnival is apparent the next day as they all are led by Dick the ringmaster to see Abe North off at the train. The three women seem to spring like monkeys and to perch on his shoulders, the crown of his hat, or the gold head of his cane as he conducts them into the station pointing out its wonders. As they stand talking, gunshots punctuate their holiday. A friend of Nicole's has shot a man in some undefined argument, and when Nicole and Rosemary look to Dick to make a moral comment, he is unable to relate this violence to the world he has created, and their carnival mood is shattered.

The crisis of the conflict between Dick and Nicole appropriately occurs at a country fair in a scene which is a gloss of "A Night at the Fair," the Basil story which reveals the origin of the carnival imagery in an incident from Fitzgerald's youth. Nicole's mask, her "sudden awful smile," is evident as she becomes absorbed in the excitement of the harlequinade midway where colorful peasant dress and display wagons form a gaudy background for the "whining, tinkling, hootchy-kootchy show." Father Schwartz's warning about heat and sweat is echoed as Nicole runs from Dick, for "the hot afternoon went shrill and terrible with her flight" (189); and as Dick pursues her, he finds himself circling the merry-go-round in a dizzying parody of its aimless motion. He finds her on the Ferris wheel laughing hysterically because she imagines that Dick had been flirting with a fifteen-year-old girl in the crowd. She pleads for Dick's help, and he is profoundly moved, for he cannot watch her disintegrations without participating in them. They return to the children "with a hot sorrow streaming down upon them" (191), both irreparably marked by the heat and the sweat of the carnival.

Later, when Dick meets Rosemary in Rome on his way back to Zurich after his father's death, he perversely punishes himself by betraying Nicole with this child. As he waits in his hotel room for Rosemary to be free, the carnival is suggested to him by the sunlight that plays in the room "with a jingling of old brass rings" (207). And after their affair has been consummated, Dick seeks punishment in a public brawl and is beaten by Italian policemen wearing harlequin hats.

Back on the Riviera for the denouement of their marriage, the carnival trappings on the beach—the trapezes and swinging rings, the portable bathhouses and floating towers, the searchlights from last night's party—form an ironic setting for the Divers' present state and their memories of the past. Nicole knows that, fortified with a drink or two, Dick would have fumbled through the stunts on the swinging rings he had once done with ease for her. In fact, in a childish regression, he does attempt to re-create the past with his embarrassing exhibition on the aquaplane. In the scene in which Barban makes Dick realize that Nicole will leave him, Dick is preoccupied with a symbolic parade which passes their cafe table.

> First was a lone cyclist in a red jersey, toiling intent and confident out of the westering sun, passing to the melody of a high chattering cheer. Then three together in a harlequinade of faded color, legs caked yellow with dust and sweat, faces expressionless, eyes heavy and endlessly tired. (309-10)

Once fresh, colorful, vital, and promising in life's race, now (the color gone from the carnival) Dick is weary and numb with the endless trying to lead the parade.

The Diver marriage over and his life effectively ended, Dick takes leave of his creation, the Carnival by the Sea, in an appropriate priestly gesture; he stands swaying on his terrace, and with his right hand he traces a papal cross on the "tan prayer rug of a beach" below. The lost members of his flock look to him from under their now cruelly harlequinade umbrellas, and Nicole, in an automatic response to his gesture, rises to her knees to go to him. The carnival has rejected its ringmaster; the flock has defrocked its priest; but, true to his misconceived role, Dick—drunken and shattered as he is by their opportunistic abuse—leaves them as he must, with a grotesque benediction.

Of all of his heroes, Fitzgerald considered Dick Diver his "comparatively good brother," and in telling his story, Fitgerald revealed all of the terror of their family's history: the son failed by father and Church wilfully rejecting his spiritual endowment; and the man who allowed himself to be emasculated by masked female destroyers, irretrievably damned by his choice of a life of folly in the carnival of the City of Man.

5.

The Last Years: 1935-1940

The six years that remained of Fitzgerald's life after *Tender Is the Night* was published were desperate ones in which he tried merely to survive. In the spring of 1935, he went to a small town in North Carolina to try to cure himself of his drinking problem. It was a bitter and solitary time in which old alliances and sources of strength broke down. Hemingway had called him a "rummy" and had told him that he had lost respect for him as a serious writer. John Peale Bishop had called him a social climber in a magazine piece, and it was clear to him that both Max Perkins and Harold Ober considered him a hopeless alcoholic.[1] His friendship with Tony Buttitta, a young aspiring writer and the proprietor of a small bookshop in Asheville, and his affair with a married woman were, respectively, moderative and disquieting components of his emotional life. With Buttitta he cried easily, especially when he was reminded of the gay times with Zelda. He confessed that he blamed himself for her breakdown and that he regretted not having died at thirty when he was at the top of his profession. And although he was flattered by the adoration of his lover, whom he called "Rosemary" because she reminded him of that character in *Tender Is the Night,* he drank excessively to block his puritan conscience. Buttitta observes that there "was a specifically Catholic cast to that conscience." [2] Fitzgerald told his young confessor that he had considered the priesthood and that since his boyhood he had been frightened of his sensuality, which he had tried to ignore or curb, "imbued as he was with the concept of the flesh as sinful and evil." [3]

The "cure" did not work, and he described these months of his breakdown, which was precipitated by years of dissipation, in the three confessional articles he wrote for *Esquire*.[4] Fitzgerald attempted to absolve himself of his sins in these essays, which he called his "gloom articles," and they constitute his late spiritual autobiography. They are a remarkable record of a man's self-lacerating examination of conscience, a stark look at the "real dark night of the soul [where] it is always three o'clock in the morning day after day" ("Handle With Care" [75]). Here we find Fitzgerald's own rationale for the prominence of certain themes in his work: the inevitability of failure, his ambivalence about money, emotional bankruptcy, the female destroyer, failed paternity, and his profession of faith in his function as a writer.

Confessional Pieces and Letters

In "The Crack-Up" (February 1936) he describes life as a process of breaking down in which the decisive blows seem to come from outside oneself, but in reality they come from within and are not felt until it is too late. He had known as a young man that he would never have the power of a man of strong political or religious convictions, and he had been able to function only by holding in precarious balance his sense of the futility of effort and his sense of the necessity to struggle. He admits that he had been only a mediocre caretaker of the resources of his talent in not keeping to the line he had found in *The Great Gatsby*, in the years when he dissipated his energy in high living, and in his writing slick-magazine fiction to support the sort of life that had nothing to do with the needs of an artist. He realizes that for years he had drawn upon resources he did not have, that he had mortaged himself physically and spiritually to the limit. In the confessional of this article he pronounces his *mea culpas*, but he also implies a prior weakness in himself for which he perhaps is not responsible. He likens himself to a plate that had cracked under pressure, and he obliquely implies that if the material had been properly composed and fired into lasting strength at the beginning, it could have withstood any punishment. He finds himself without vitality, but, he implies, that was the fault of his meager patrimony: "You have it or you haven't it, like health or brown eyes or honor or a baritone voice" (69). He had failed to be prudent and wise, but, as he saw it all his life, Edward and Mollie Fitzgerald must share in his failures. He referred to another influential element of his past as he ends this first installment of his *apologia pro vita sua* with the quotation from Matthew [5-13]: "Ye are the salt of the earth. But if the salt hath lost its savour, wherewith shall it be salted?"

Fitzgerald acknowledged in "Handle With Care" (March 1936) that some would find the self-revelation of these articles contemptible unless he ended them with thanks to the gods for his Unconquerable Soul. But, he asserts, he had been thanking them for too long for nothing, and now he wants to put a lament into his record. This "cracked plate's further history" continues with an elaboration of the metaphor: the defective plate must be kept in service as a household necessity, but it cannot bear careless handling. He feels that his personality is disintegrating, and to place his current predicament in perspective, he recalls incidents from the past, two of which had to do with a woman—his visit to a prostitute in his junior year at Princeton and his break with Zelda just after his separation from the army. The man who married the same girl a year later with the jingle of money in his pocket had acquired an enduring distrust and animosity for the wealthy, and he had always since thought that a *droit de seigneur* might have stolen Zelda from him. Consequently, he had always watched the carnival with an envy he could barely conceal, for the uneasy position of the outsider was his natural stance.

Fitzgerald had been through two brief, abortive attempts to succeed as a screenwriter in Hollywood in 1927 (January-March) and in 1931 (November-December). In Hollywood his personality had been eroded by its collaborative system and the indignity of impotently witnessing the subordination of the written word to another glittering but tasteless power, the commercial expediency of the studios. He felt as crippled by it as a small merchant crushed by a chain store. For all of his public confidence and the pronouncements he had made in various forums on the temper and manners of his time, there was no substantial self upon which he could organize his self-esteem. Hemingway was his artistic conscience and Edmund Wilson had been his intellectual mentor, for Fitzgerald admits that he had done little thinking beyond the problems of his craft and that his social and political consciousness had been formed by others. Now approaching his fortieth year he is like a child left alone in a big house, free to do anything he wishes, but there is nothing he wants to do, there is no excitement or capacity for pleasure in his life, and the someone who could have helped him to keep his shop open is sound asleep.

"Pasting It Together" (April 1936) is the third act of this Jazz Age Trimalchio's morality play, and while it does not offer total redemption in its denouement, it does reveal the course of Fitzgerald's temporal salvation. Many had believed in and counted upon him, and his puritanical sense of duty dictated that he examine his disease and perhaps find the preventative for them as well as restore himself to functioning good health. His identification with the objects of his disparate emotions which had meant death to accomplishment and his inability to fulfill his obligations led to thoughts of the self-immolation many of his contemporaries had either considered or acted upon. Wordsworth and Keats had experienced the passing away of glory from the earth, but they had prevailed, and Fitzgerald knew he must count himself among those who continue to be writers because they must; he must continue to be a writer because it is the only way he knows to structure and communicate experience. Momentarily he poses as a complete misanthrope who decries the wasteful giving of oneself to parasitic suppliants, his constant generosity giving the lie to his selfish resolve. But, having for the moment rejected ideals, he is finally a writer only, and he accepts the maxim that "the natural state of the sentient adult is a qualified unhappiness" (84). What he thought had been his happiness was as chimerical as the boom in the twenties, and he will now pay in isolation and calcified emotions for this new dispensation from self-lacerating involvement in the carnival.

The letters of his last five years reveal a mature reflectiveness in Fitzgerald quite unlike the confused, sometimes self-pitying bewilderment in his earlier correspondence. He seemed to have accepted his unhappy condition with a certain measure of equanimity, and he often wrote of the moral values he had formulated in his Catholic youth. This was not precisely a regression, for these values had been the underpinning of all of his years and had caused much conflict in him. Finally, saddened and ill, much older than his years in unhappy experience, he acknowledged to himself and to others what had formed and sustained him. Perhaps because of their common Catholic backgrounds, Fitzgerald had always been especially self-revelatory with John O'Hara, to whom he wrote in the tone of "Sleeping and Waking":

> Again and again in my books I have tried to imagize my regret that I have never been as good as I intended to be (and you must know that what I mean by good is . . . a personal conscience and meaning by the personal conscience yourself stripped in white midnight before your own God).[5]

In his letters to and about his daughter, Scottie, Fitzgerald revealed not only his serious and sometimes oppressive approach to parenthood but also his desire to pass on to her the most valuable part of his own moral training. In a letter to Helen Hayes, who had brought Scottie out to Hollywood for a visit and who periodically supervised her in Fitzgerald's absence, he wrote:

> Those years [childhood] can be passed without harm in some uncertainty as to where the next meal is coming from, but they can't be passed in an ethical void without serious damage to the child's soul, if that word is still in use. The human machinery which controls the sense of right, duty, self-respect, etc. must have conscious exercise before adolescence. . . .[6]

Scottie was a vivacious and gregarious girl attending school in the East during Fitzgerald's last Hollywood sojourn, and she was not as attentive to her studies as Fitzgerald would have liked. With acute hindsight he realized and lectured her endlessly on the importance of hard work in one's youth. He wanted her to "be among the best of [her] race" [7] and to believe in "the rewards for virtue . . . and the *punishments* for not fulfilling one's duties, which are doubly costly." [8] With hard-won conviction Fitzgerald told his daughter: "For premature adventure one pays an atrocious price. . . . It's in the logic of life that no young person ever 'gets away with anything. . . .' Whatever your sins are I hope you never get to justify them to yourself." [9] And with an urgency he probably felt as much for himself as for her, he told her "to devote the best and freshest part of your energies to things that will give you a happy and profitable life. There is no other time but now." [10]

Fitzgerald was alarmed by Scottie's periodic unauthorized visits with friends in Baltimore and college weekends, for he feared that her behavior signaled her going the way of her mother and he censured her bitterly at such times. After one of her lapses, he wrote to the Harold Obers, who were in effect Scottie's foster parents in the East, ". . . her circus last spring was very costly and she deserves little more than sack cloth at the present"; [11] and "If she is going to be an idler I want no part of her. I don't even want to help her to grow up into the sort of woman I loathe . . . To hell with pretty faces if there is nothing underneath." [12] But beneath the harsh words was a profound love and concern and fear that she would learn not from him but from experience that the dissipation of one's energies was not only physically, psychologically, and professionally debilitating but also violated the strong moral sense which had sustained him and which he fervently tried to communicate to her in his sermon-letters. To Mr. and Mrs. Eben Finney, Scottie's Baltimore hosts, he wrote, revealing his old-line puritanical streak: "I still believe in the strictest chaperonage . . . because my theory follows Pope's statement that evil (I am using the word in its old-fashioned sense), first looked upon as terrible, longer looked upon as tolerable, finally becomes attractive." [13]

Hollywood: The Last Tycoon

Shortly after he arrived in Hollywood for the last time, in the summer of 1937, Fitzgerald met Sheilah Graham, a young English newspaperwoman, who was to be his companion for what remained of his life. There was a striking physical resemblance between her and Zelda which Fitzgerald made an important point in *The Last Tycoon*, but Miss Graham was supportive while Zelda had been fiercely competitive, and she supplied him some measure of stability in his last years. But this relationship was not completely placid. Fitzgerald's chronic drinking problem was undoubtedly aggravated by his residual puritanical response to his affair with Miss Graham, and there were several violent moments when he viciously attacked her for her poor and adventurous past. He called her "Lilith," evidence of his periodic regression to his Augustinian view of women, and after his death she found the words "Portrait of a Prostitute" which Fitzgerald had written on the back of her picture. A temporary break between them came when he drunkenly threatened her with a gun, but they soon became reconciled, and for the year before he died he was abstemious. Fitzgerald was never completely easy in this affair for all the comfort and renewed hope it brought him. When his daughter visited from the East, he asked Miss Graham to move her clothes out of his apartment, and he told Nunnally Johnson that he supposed he would not want to visit him at home because he was living there with his paramour, a word Johnson thought identified Fitzgerald as a Methodist until his wife told him that he was a Catholic.

Since Fitzgerald did not live to complete *The Last Tycoon*, it cannot be considered a finished, coherent work. But we do have six substantial chapters as well as his extensive notes on the rest, enough to view it as a mature statement of his experience and art. Fitzgerald went at the composition of *The Last Tycoon* with the resolve and confidence with which he approached the material of *The Great Gatsby*, for the protracted turmoil and painful effort which yielded *Tender Is the Night* was behind him. We cannot know, of course, what changes he might have made in the serial and book manuscripts of *The Last Tycoon*, [14] but what we do have is consistent with the leading themes, patterns of characterization, stylistic devices, and evidence of his residual Catholic consciousness in the great body of his work.

Like Gatsby, Stahr is a protean mythic figure. He can assume at will various roles:—"one of the boys," director, cameraman, businessman, lover, father, and miraculous healer. In him are combined both the qualities of a pagan mythical figure like Daedalus and of Christ. A skilled artisan, he had soared on strong wings, staying aloft longer than most could, and with eyes that could stare straight into the sun he regarded all of earth's kingdoms and then settled gradually to earth remembering everything he had seen. He is described as both an oracle and "a proud young shepherd" who saw in the medium of film a new way to measure man's hopes, rogueries, and sorrows, and he has come to Hollywood by choice "to stay with us to the end" (20). As a boy he had wanted to be a chief clerk who knew where everything was, and this is his function in the empire he has created, where he possesses everything and everyone. When he is observed at the studio by a group of visiting Knights of Columbus, their reverent gaze is riveted on him, for they had seen the Host carried in processions, but he is the Incarnation. With malice Brady refers to Stahr as "that goddamn Vine Street Jesus" (103); and one of Cecilia's fellow sanitarium inmates, in response to her idealized account of Stahr, asks if he were "Christ in Industry" (145). Furthermore, when Stahr agreed to help an actor's fading career by publicly showing his favor, the "man ascended into Heaven" (162). But Stahr is an unworthy father and a travesty of Christ in his inability or refusal to choose worthy and generous images instead of the tawdry and manipulative images he uses.

The prominent failed father in the novel is Brady, father to Cecilia, the Irish Catholic chronicler of the novel's action. Brady is a transplanted bar boy from Ballyhegan, but he has been able to give his daughter the sort of Continental education experienced by Beatrice O'Hara Blaine. Cecilia, who has attended a convent school where, against heavy odds, she managed to be the only virgin, has apparently absorbed a code other than her father's. She is, like Nick Carraway, the embodiment of a puritanical and established morality, which emerges in her observations of her father's and Stahr's activities. Cecilia uses the language of her Catholic orientation in describing her relationship to Hollywood; she notes that even before she had reached the age of reason she had been in a position to watch the wheels of the Hollywood carousel go round. And she knows with the certitude of one who has known solid Irish Catholic guilt that what usually makes a good story is what people are ashamed of.

The world of *The Last Tycoon* is a vast carnival in the American mode, and Monroe Stahr is the apotheosis of the supreme and judgmental ringmaster who sees the sham of the world he has created even though he is committed to perpetuating it. He is, in fact, a purveyor of the meretricious images of the City of Man to those who cannot discern the essential difference between the sacred and the profane. He puts his writers through their paces as they dutifully prance in the circle he circumscribes, and the gagman Mike Van Dyke performs his Keystone routine at the imaginary and instructive shot of Stahr's gun. Wylie White, the screenwriter who pursues Cecilia as much for her father's influence as for herself, an outsider in this "mining town in lotus land" (11), sees the corrupt reality beneath Hollywood's lush exterior. It is a place where green moss can be bought for two dollars an inch for a garden party and where he feels he has no rightful identity until a hotel clerk hands him a letter addressed to him in his name and where, according to its perverse class-oriented moral code, a woman with whom he has had an affair can threaten to have her producer husband throw him out of Hollywood if he should talk about it.

Cecilia says that her father has acquired a quarter interest in "a booming circus," just as Josep Bloeckman, the film entrepreneur and Anthony Patch's rival for Gloria in *The Beautiful and Damned* had started as a peanut vendor and then progressed to the master of a carnival sideshow. The heat and the sweat and the life, the correlative of the essential corruption of life's carnival against which Father Schwartz warned Jay Gatsby, is prevalent in the six chapters we have of *The Last Tycoon* and Fitzgerald's notes on the rest of the novel. In the scene in which Kathleen discovers her father with his secretary, there are repeated mentions of heat and sweat. Brady's shirt is soaked through with sweat, and when, having heard a moan, Kathleen opens the closet door, a naked woman tumbles out, "with her came a gust of stifling, stuffy air" (102), and she lies on the floor bathed in sweat. Stahr was to have stopped off in Washington on his trip east, and in his notes for this chapter, which Fitzgerald called "The Circus" in the outline, there is a profusion of heat images: the city is stifling; Stahr wanders around "in a daze of fever and heat" (129); back in Hollywood, in the section Fitzgerald titled "The Underworld," Stahr resumes his affair with Kathleen "during an overpowering heat wave in the early part of September" (131); and there is a "sense of heat all through" (143).

It is impossible to know if Fitzgerald would have retained these elements in the finished novel, but it is improbable that he would have abandoned the themes and points of style which were such important characteristics of his work or that he could have expunged from his art the Catholic consciousness which is evident even in this last, unfinished novel.

Scott Fitzgerald was ever acutely aware of his mortality. A man who lived so frenetic a public life and who in private often fought not to succumb to the dark night of the soul had faced the awesome inevitability more often and truly than most. Before death came he had made known his wishes about his funeral and burial both in conversation and legal document.

After his father died, Fitzgerald often said that he wanted to be buried with him and his family in the Catholic St. Mary's Cemetery at Rockville, Maryland, because "it was very friendly leaving him there with all his relations around him." [15] Optimistic about his financial future in Hollywood when he made his will in 1937, Fitzgerald stipulated that "Part of my estate is first to provide for a funeral in keeping with my station in life." Later when it became clear that the vagaries of his employers would not allow him to amass a fortune, as he had hoped, he replaced "for a funeral" with "the cheapest funeral" and added, "The same to be without undue ostentation or unnecessary expense." [16]

Even though he had made preparations, Fitzgerald was hardly ready to die. In his work on *The Last Tycoon* he knew that he had found his novelist's voice again and that he was creating a work of the economy and power of *The Great Gatsby*. He was excited about his new novel, and the work was going well when a second heart attack killed him and ended his dream of personal and artistic vindication.

Fitzgerald had not been ready for his death in another respect.

In order for a Catholic to be buried in consecrated ground with the rites of the Church, he must have been in a "state of grace" at the time of his death. To achieve this he must have been a practicing Catholic, have received final absolution from a priest, confessed his guilt and asked for forgiveness on his own, or received absolution even after his death. The latter is made possible by the Church's concession that absolution can be given until that time when all life has left the body. Although this is a clinical or medical matter, the Church has set a general limit of three hours after death. Not one of these conditions had been met in Fitzgerald's case. We know that he had ceased to practice his religion almost twenty years before, and a priest was not summoned either before or after his death. In her affective account in *Beloved Infidel,* Sheilah Graham tells us that she and Fitzgerald were alone when he abruptly lost consciousness and died within a few minutes, and in the confusion that ensued she lost control of the situation. That it would not have occurred to her to call for a priest is evident in her letter to Fitzgerald's daughter written a few weeks later. One of his relatives had asked Miss Graham if a priest had been with Fitzgerald at the end. She replied that it had been too sudden for such considerations, but she told Scottie, "I didn't tell her that Scott had abandoned the Catholic religion years ago and was definitely against all that sort of thing." [17] Nevertheless, in accordance with his wishes, shortly after his death Fitzgerald's body was sent from California to Baltimore and then on to the Pumphry Funeral Home in Bethesda, Maryland. There he waited in silent appeal like Gatsby while a few friends tried to arrange the burial he had requested.

In his account of the circumstances of Fitzgerald's burial in *The Far Side of Paradise,* Arthur Mizener created a bit of mythology that has endured for over twenty years. Mizener said that Fitzgerald was refused burial in St. Mary's Cemetery because "his books were proscribed and he had not died a good Catholic." [18] The latter is certainly true, but, in fact, Fitzgerald's books have never been proscribed by the Catholic Church. Andrew Turnbull did not repeat the error in his biography, where he states the case thus: "Fitzgerald had wanted to be buried with his family in the

Catholic cemetery in Rockville, but since he had died a non-believer, the bishop raised objections, and he was buried in the Union Cemetery not far away." [19] Unfortunately, Mizener's rationale has been stated without documentation in subsequent books by Kenneth Eble, [20] Nancy Milford, [21] and Sara Mayfield, [22] and in a recent newspaper feature article.[23]

Mizener based his assertion that Fitzgerald's books were proscribed on the narrative of one of the men involved in arranging the burial, John Biggs, who was Fitzgerald's Princeton roommate.[24] Judge Biggs with Eben Finney, who had also known Fitzgerald at school, and Fitzgerald's lawyer, Edgar Poe, made repeated requests to the office of Archbishop Michael Curley, the bishop of Baltimore, for permission to give Fitzgerald a Catholic burial. At this late date Judge Biggs can recall only that he was told by a monsignor in the bishop's office that Fitzgerald would not be allowed a Catholic funeral because his writings were undesirable and because he had not made his Easter duty.[25] "Easter duty" refers to a Catholic's obligation each year to receive the sacraments of Penance and Communion within the six weeks before and the eight weeks after Easter Sunday. If one does not fulfill this requisite, he is in a state of excommunication.

Although Mizener, Turnbull, and Mayfield attribute the refusal of a Catholic burial to the bishop, there is no hard evidence to support this view. Since Scott Fitzgerald's name does not appear in the records of Archbishop Curley's administration and since there is nothing concerning either the censure of his books or the difficulties of his burial, [26] it is not clear that the archbishop was even involved in this matter. It is possible that he either privately felt that Fitzgerald's writings were undesirable or that he publicly denounced them from his pulpit, but he never took any official action against them, nor has any other churchman, for Fitzgerald has never been listed in the *Index Librorum Prohibitorum*.

All appeals denied, Fitzgerald's friends arranged a service for him not without its ironies. They found a young, newly ordained Episcopal minister, the Reverend Raymond P. Black, who was willing to officiate. When he was told who the deceased was, he said "it made no particular difference to [him]" who it was.[27] Mr.

Black conducted the brief service at the chapel, and Andrew Turnbull, who was present, observed that "It was as if nothing were being said of him or *to* him that the heart could hear." [28] Then, as if in cruel parody of Gatsby's obsequies, the mourners drove in the rain at dusk to Rockville Cemetery, where the simple Episcopal graveside rite was intoned. Dorothy Parker had earlier echoed the benediction of Owl-eyes for Gatsby which was painfully appropriate: "The poor son-of-a-bitch."

Fitzgerald's wish to be buried next to his father was finally granted on November 8, 1975, when he along with Zelda was reinterred in St. Mary's Cemetery at a ceremony conducted by the pastor of St. Mary's, the Reverend William J. Silk, who spoke of Fitzgerald's intimate knowledge and portrayal of human imperfection in his work. What was in 1940 a quiet country cemetery—of which Fitzgerald said, "I wouldn't mind a bit if in a few years Zelda and I could snuggle up together [here] under a stone. . . . That is really a happy thought and not melancholy at all" [29]—now lies at the intersection of two four-lane highways in what has become a suburb of Washington, D.C. When Fitzgerald's daughter learned that the cemetery had been designated a historic landmark and would be preserved from further encroachment, she asked for and received approval to have her parents removed from Rockville Cemetery to St. Mary's. Reinterment was granted by William Cardinal Baum, archbishop of Washington, an ecumenicist and one of a new breed of churchmen who are not so concerned with the technicalities which prevented Fitzgerald's burial there thirty-five years before.[30] The fact that Cardinal Baum allowed Zelda Fitzgerald to be buried in consecrated ground with her husband is startling and refreshing evidence that the Church, which is now willing to claim Fitzgerald as her own, has changed.

The statement which Cardinal Baum issued on the occasion of the reinterment is an expression of reconciliation and recognition of the profound moral sense of Fitzgerald's life and work.

F. Scott Fitzgerald came out of the Maryland Catholic tradition. He was a man touched by the faith of the Catholic Church. There can be perceived in his work a Catholic consciousness of reality. He found in this faith an understanding of the human heart caught in the struggle between grace and death. His characters are involved in this great drama, seeking God and seeking love. As an artist he was able with lucidity and poetic imagination to portray this struggle. He also experienced in his own life the mystery of suffering and, we hope, the power of God's grace.[31]

Notes

Introduction

1. F. Scott Fitzgerald, "The Notebooks," *The Crack-Up,* ed. Edmund Wilson (New York, 1956), p. 277. Hereafter cited as "Notebooks" and *The Crack-Up.*

Chapter 1

1. Clara Hill Lindley, ed. *Some Letters of Monsignor Louis E. Caillet and August N. Chemidlin 1868-1899* (St. Paul, 1922), p. 9.
2. Sister Margaret Mary Burke to Joan M. Allen (hereafter cited as JMA), 7 September 1971.
3. Kathryn G. Boardman, "F. Scott Fitzgerald's Sister Annabell Makes Final Visit to Home City," *St. Paul Pioneer Press,* 22 August 1971, p. 28.
4. That Fitzgerald was aware of the subtle difference is apparent in a clipping from a St. Paul newspaper in his scrapbook. The picture shows the old McQuillan mansion which had been converted into a hospital. In the caption, Fitzgerald had inserted the word "wholesale" in the phrase which refers to his grandfather, "a pioneer grocery dealer of St. Paul." F. Scott Fitzgerald Papers, Princeton University. Hereafter cited as Fitzgerald Papers.
5. Matthew J. Bruccoli to JMA, 3 December 1971.
6. Sister Kathleen, Holy Angels School, to JMA, 25 June 1971.
7. *F. Scott Fitzgerald's Ledger: A Facsimile,* Intro. Matthew J. Bruccoli (Washington, D.C., 1972). Hereafter cited as *Ledger.*

8. Vicar General Andrew P. Mahoney, Oblates of Mary Immaculate, to JMA, 14 December 1971.

9. Margaret Benner, D.H.M., to JMA, 2 March 1972.

10. Citations from "That Kind of Party" are to *The Basil and Josephine Stories,* eds. John Kuehl and Jackson Bryer (New York, 1973).

11. Annabel writes today: "Scott and I were so different that I guess he did not accomplish much in the line of making me a belle." Annabel F. Sprague to JMA, 18 January 1972.

12. Fitzgerald Papers.

13. Edith in "May Day" (1920) is a "pretty doll . . . as if you touched her she'd smear" *(Stories,* 85), and "Her lips were finely made of deep carmine; the irises of her eyes were delicate, breakable blue, like China eyes" (99).

The smile of the heroine of "Winter Dreams" (1922) is "blatantly artificial" *(Stories,* 128), and "the color in her cheeks was centred [sic] like the color in a picture" (132). She is "a slender enamelled doll in cloth of gold" (140).

Ailie Calhoun, "The Last of the Belles" (1929), wears "too much fever-colored rouge . . . accentuated by a nose dabbed clownish white" *(Stories,* 122).

Josephine, the heroine of "First Blood" (1930), has a "mouth twisted into a universal sympathy . . . the expression not of a victim, but rather of the very *demon* of tender melancholy" *(Taps at Reveille* [New York, 1934], 122).

Other stories in which this pattern is prominent are "The Debutante" (1917), "The Sensible Thing" (1924), "The Adjuster" (1925), "The Rough Crossing" (1929), and "The Bridal Party" (1930).

14. F. Scott Fitzgerald, *The Letters of F. Scott Fitzgerald,* ed. Andrew Turnbull (New York, 1966), p. 467. Hereafter cited as *Letters.*

15. Edward Fitzgerald to FSF, 30 July 1909, Scrapbook, Fitzgerald Papers.

16. See Michel Mok, "The Other Side of Paradise," *New York Post,* 25 September 1936. Reprinted in *F. Scott Fitzgerald in His Own Time: A Miscellany,* eds. Matthew J. Bruccoli and Jackson R. Bryer (Kent, 1971).

17. *Letters,* p. 474.

18. *Ledger,* p. 163.

19. *Letters,* p. 617.

20. *Ledger,* p. 163.

21. "The Death of My Father," Fitzgerald Papers.

22. F. Scott Fitzgerald, "The Notebooks," *The Crack-Up,* p. 211. An allusion to two characters in Thackeray's *Vanity Fair.*

23. Citations from "Shadow Laurels" are to *Apprentice Fiction of F. Scott Fitzgerald 1909-1917,* ed. John Kuehl (New Brunswick, 1965).

24. Lindley, p. 24.

25. "Father Busch" was the Reverend Joseph F. Busch, who in 1905

had been superior of the Diocesan Mission Band and in the year of Fitzgerald's citation was appointed bishop of Lead and in 1915 bishop of St. Cloud.

26. Arthur Mizener to JMA, 7 December 1971.

27. Patricia McLaughlin, Cathedral of St. Paul, to JMA, 31 August 1971.

28. John Kuehl, "Scott Fitzgerald's 'Thoughtbook,' " *Princeton University Library Chronicle,* 26 (Winter 1965), 102.

29. "Notebooks," p. 121.

30. James Michael Reardon, *The Catholic Church in the Diocese of St. Paul* (St. Paul, 1952), pp. 24, 27.

31. Ibid., p. 24.

32. J. F. Powers, "Cross-Country—St. Paul, Home of the Saints," *Partisan Review,* 16 (July, 1949), 717.

33. *Letters,* p. 355.

34. "Notebooks," p. 234.

35. Ibid., p. 240.

36. Citations from "A Night at the Fair" are to *Afternoon of an Author,* ed. Arthur Mizener (New York, 1957).

37. *Ledger,* p. 163.

38. The Newman School's tuition was in the upper range of the schools in the area. In 1917 its fee was $900. Porter Sargent, *A Handbook of American Private Schools* (New York, 1918), p. 348.

39. Andrew Turnbull, *Scott Fitzgerald* (New York, 1962), p. 34.

40. Joseph M. Flynn, *The Catholic Church in New Jersey* (Morristown, 1914), p. 372.

41. Dumas Malone, ed., *Dictionary of American Biography,* Vol. IV (New York, 1961), p. 495.

42. Newman School Brochure, Collection of JMA.

43. Henry Dan Piper, *F. Scott Fitzgerald: A Critical Portrait* (New York, 1965), p. 16.

44. There are no Newman School archives, no hard information about its curriculum, but Fitzgerald's transcript indicates that in his two years at the school he took five Latin courses. He also studied English, American, and ancient history; French; algebra, plane and solid geometry; and physics—a solid and traditional American curriculum.

45. Sargent, p. 160.

46. Malone, p. 274.

47. Sargent, p. 601.

48. Realtor's Appraisal of Newman School, Lakewood, New Jersey, Collection of JMA.

49. "Newman School Closes Friday," *The Evening Record and Bergen County Herald,* 3 June 1913, p. 1.

50. "Reception for Cardinal Gibbons/Baltimore Prelate Expected at Newman School for Brief Visit This Afternoon," *The Bergen Evening Record,* 4 May 1914, p. 1.

51. "Cardinal Gibbons Made Visit to Newman Shool," *The Bergen Evening Record*, 5 May 1914, p. 1.

52. "Newman and Hume Schools to Be Combined," *The Bergen Evening Record*, 25 July 1912, p. 1.

53. "Newman School Overcrowded This Year," *The Bergen Evening Record*, 25 September 1912, p. 2.

54. Sargent, p. 348.

55. "Newman School Students Vied Weekly for Spot on Corner," *The Bergen Evening Record*, 1 October 1935, p. 36.

56. Turnbull, p. 33.

57. "Henry Ford Pays Visit to Sick Newman Boys," *The Bergen Evening Record*, 21 April 1914, p. 1.

58. Stanley J. Kunitz and Howard Haycraft, eds., *Twentieth Century Authors* (New York, 1942), pp. 291-92.

59. Citations from "The Freshest Boy" are to *Taps at Reveille* (New York, 1934).

60. Years later Fitzgerald was still sensitive on this point. Among the biographical data he was asked to supply for an alumni directory, he included the statement that his father "was a broker before he retired." Newman School, Alumni Directory (May 1930), p. 10, Fitzgerald Papers.

61. F. Scott Fitzgerald, "Author's House," *Afternoon of an Author*, p. 186.

62. Citations from "The Perfect Life" are to *Taps at Reveille*.

63. "Notebooks," p. 239.

64. Fitzgerald Papers.

65. Frank Willing Leach, "The Philadelphia of Our Ancestors: Old Philadelphia Families—LXIV—Hutchinson," *The North American*, 23 August 1908, Sunday Supplement, p. 1.

66. Capt. Alfred Forbes Fay to Brig. Gen. L. Thomas, Adjt. Gen., U.S.A., 8 June 1865.

67. Affidavit of Sigourney W. Fay, 14 April 1885.

68. Capt. Alfred Forbes Fay to Brig. Gen. L. Thomas, Adjt. Gen., U.S.A., 8 June 1865.

69. Fay Affidavit, 14 April 1885.

70. The documents cited in notes 66-69 and the information used to detail Fay's army career are from his Military Service and Pension Records in the National Archives, Washington, D.C.

71. R. C. Nevius, "A Note on F. Scott Fitzgerald's Monsignor Sigourney Fay and His Early Career as an Episcopalian," *Fitzgerald/Hemingway Annual 1971*, eds. Matthew J. Bruccoli and C. E. Frazer Clark, Jr. (Washington, D.C., 1971), p. 106.

72. Ibid., pp 111-12.

73. Scrapbook, Fitzgerald Papers.

74. Margaret Chanler, *Autumn in the Valley* (Boston, 1936), p. 50.

75. Ibid., p. 72.

76. Ibid., pp. 78-79.

150 NOTES

77. Ibid., pp. 84-85.
78. R.P. Blackmur, "Henry Adams: Three Late Moments," *Kenyon Review*, 2 (Winter 1940), 24.
79. Worthington Chauncey Ford, ed., *Letters of Henry Adams (1892-1918)*, Vol. 2 (Boston, 1938), p. 630.
80. Cyril Sigourney W. Fay, *The Bride of the Lamb and Other Essays* (New York, 1922), p. ix.
81. F. Scott Fitzgerald, "Homage to the Victorians," *New York Tribune*, 14 May 1922, IV, p. 7.
82. Shane Leslie, "Review of *This Side of Paradise*," *Dublin Review*, 167 (1920), 287.
83. Nevius, p. 106.
84. Jesse Albert Locke to FSF, 26 November 1933, Fitzgerald Papers.
85. F. Scott Fitzgerald, "Wait Till You Have Children of Your Own," *Woman's Home Companion* (July, 1924), p. 105.
86. Hugh A. Kennedy to JMA, 3 December 1971.
87. T. B. Chetwood, S.J., "Father Thomas J. Delihant, S.J. 1878-1949," *Woodstock Letters*, 78 (1949), pp. 351-54.
88. Arthur Mizener, *The Far Side of Paradise* (Boston, 1965), p. 41.
89. Citations from "The Ordeal" are to *Apprentice Fiction of F. Scott Fitzgerald 1909-1917*.
90. Turnbull, p. 37.
91. Citations from "Benediction" are to *Flappers and Philosophers* (New York, 1920).
92. *Letters*, p. 403.
93. Fitzgerald Papers.
94. Shane Leslie, "Memories of Scott Fitzgerald," [London] *Times Literary Supplement*, 21 November 1958, p. 673.
95. Fitzgerald probably would not have been very disturbed by Hemmick's ultimate rejection of him. In a conspiratorial tone, Monsignor Fay wrote his response to Fitzgerald's classification of types in this statement of qualification. "I should take as the first type ourselves; the second class Leslie; the third class Father Hemmick; fourth class Mr. Delbos [the successor to Fay as Headmaster of the Newman School]. . . ." Sigourney Fay to FSF, 4 October 1917, Fitzgerald Papers.
96. "Monsignor William Hemmick Dies in Rome," *New York Times*, 21 September 1971, II, p. 40.
97. Shane Leslie, "Memories," p. 673.
98. Shane Leslie, "Some Memories of Scott Fitzgerald," [London] *Times Literary Supplement*, 31 October 1958, p. 632.
99. Turnbull, p. 338.
100. John Tracy Ellis, *The Life of James Cardinal Gibbons*, Vol. II (Milwaukee, 1952), pp. 266-67.
101. Ellis, pp. 267, 280.

102. Sigourney Fay to FSF, no date, Fitzgerald Papers.

103. Ellis, p. 278.

104. Fay to FSF, [Rome], no date, Fitzgerald Papers.

105. Fay to FSF, 6 June 1918, Fitzgerald Papers.

106. F. Scott Fitzgerald, "The Crack-Up," *The Crack-Up,* p. 69.

107. F. Scott Fitzgerald, "A Woman of the Past," *Taps at Reveille,* p. 153.

108. Elizabeth Beckwith Mackie, "My Friend Scott Fitzgerald," *Fitzgerald/Hemingway Annual 1970* (Washington, D.C., 1970), pp. 20-21.

109. Turnbull, p. 69.

110. Fitzgerald Papers.

111. Arthur Mizener, *The Far Side of Paradise* (Boston, 1965) p. 65.

112. F. Scott Fitzgerald, "Handle With Care," *The Crack-Up,* p. 76.

113. Ernest Boyd, *Portraits: Real and Imaginary* (New York, 1924), pp. 220-21.

Chapter 2

1. Citations from "Sentiment and the Use of Rouge" are to *Apprentice Fiction.*

2. *Letters,* p. 469.

3. Turnbull, p. 339.

4. F. Scott Fitzgerald, *F. Scott Fitzgerald in His Own Time: A Miscellany,* eds. M. J. Bruccoli and Jackson R. Bryer (Kent, 1971), pp. 115-16.

5. Shane Leslie, "Some Memories of Scott Fitzgerald," [London] *Times Literary Supplement,* 31 October 1958, p. 632.

6. Ibid.

7. Leslie, *Long Shadows* (London, 1966), p. 251.

8. Perhaps one can excuse Leslie's exaggeration of his role in Fitzgerald's career and his distortion of fact. Successful people have always attracted this sort of self-serving comment, but one cannot so easily forgive Leslie's backbiting and simple lack of kindness in recent years. He was not alone in thinking that Fitzgerald's extraordinary early success was unwarranted; but few, on one hand, claim that *This Side of Paradise,* presumably because of some grammatical corrections one made in an early manuscript, is Fitzgerald's finest book and, on the other hand, dispute Fitzgerald's claim to a solid critical reputation. In derisive tone, Leslie has said, "Princeton ... probably to the huge amusement of Monsignor Fay and other friends in the next world, has seriously collected Fitzgerald together with its other great alumnus, Woodrow Wilson!" *(Times Literary Supplement,* 31 October 1958, p. 632). One wonders at the lack of humanity in this statement: "Poor darlings—they slowly descended like spoiled children until their ghastly ends years later: She was burned alive in a bughouse and he scraped out the last flicker of his talent as a Hollywood hack." *(Long Shadows* [London, 1966], p. 252.)

9. Shane Leslie to FSF, 9 September 1918, Fitzgerald Papers.

10. Leslie, *Long Shadows*, p. 249.

11. Sigourney Fay to FSF, 6 June 1918, Fitzgerald Papers.

12. Sara Mayfield, *Exiles from Paradise* (New York, 1971), p. 3.

13. Margaret Chanler, *Autumn in the Valley* (Boston, 1936), p. 85.

14. Shane Leslie to FSF, 23 January 1919, Fitzgerald Papers.

15. Milton Stern in *The Golden Moment: The Novels of F. Scott Fitzgerald* (Urbana, 1970) uses this as evidence to discount the importance of Catholicism in Fitzgerald's imagination and work. In a paragraph concerning *This Side of Paradise*, he says, ". . . for Fitzgerald Catholicism belonged to the gorgeous adolescent dreamworld of rich appearances" (p. 49). While Fitzgerald's attraction to the rich appearances of Catholicism and especially the glamorous possibilities of the Church opened up to him by Fay is certainly part of the picture, it is just that—a part of a complex element of the making of Fitzgerald's imagination.

Stern supports his contention that Fitzgerald did not feel himself a Catholic with his citation of a 1925 letter from Italy to Ernest Boyd in which Fitzgerald said, "We're tired of black skirts [sic] and dirty teeth and the parades of Pope Siphilis the Sixth. . . ." (Fitzgerald Papers; *Letters*, p. 496.) There are several problems with Stern's interpretation. If Stern means to imply that "black skirts" refers to priests' cassocks, then this point of his argument is exploded, for he has misread a key word. The word in question in both the Turnbull transcription and in the original letter is *shirt*, not skirt, and it was probably the Fascisti of which the Fitzgeralds had grown tired. Apparently Stern also considers the papal name evidence of Fitzgerald's disavowal of Catholicism. He forgets that the insider is allowed latitude in his humor, and it is likely that Fitzgerald was merely trying for a bit of humorous alliteration.

Stern claims that "the combination of tone, intention, biography—a general sense of what Fitzgerald was like" (p. 48)—influences his conclusions. Yet he ignores the facetious tone and context of the remark he cites. Ernest Boyd had written a sketch in his *Portraits: Real and Imaginary* which emphasized the capricious public life the Fitzgeralds had lived in New York and Paris. In the "breezy" tone of Fitzgerald's letter, which Stern notes, he was attempting to match Boyd's tone. Fitzgerald tended to clown and pose in his letters, and surely this was the case in this letter.

Kenneth Eble in *F. Scott Fitzgerald* (New Haven, 1963) cites this Ledger entry to support his contention that Amory Blaine's inability to accept Catholicism represents Fitzgerald's "definite and permanent separation from the Church" (p. 50). Yet Eble, unlike Stern, concedes that "the moral concern and the sense of evil to be found in all his serious work may be important consequences of his youthful religious interest" (p. 58).

16. *Letters*, p. 60.

17. Charles G. Shaw, "F. Scott Fitzgerald," *F. Scott Fitzgerald in His Own Time: A Miscellany*, p. 283.

18. One of them is among Fitzgerald's books at Princeton, a highly technical book, *Scientific Theism versus Materialism: The Space-Time Potential* by Arvid Reuterdahl. Mrs. Fitzgerald's inscription reflects the troubled interplay between them: "F. S. Fitz, from Mother, To be fair—Please read—Strongly recommended—."

19. Edmund Wilson to FSF, 9 August 1919, Fitzgerald Papers.

20. *Letters*, p. 349.

21. Mayfield (New York, 1971), p. 53.

22. Sara Mayfield to JMA, 8 August 1971.

23. Desmond J. Vella, Archdiocese of New York, to JMA, 28 September 1971.

24. Mizener, p. 119.

25. Citations from "The Romantic Egoist" are to the typescript. Fitzgerald Papers.

26. Citations from "An Author's House" are to *Afternoon of an Author.*

27. Citations from the text are to *This Side of Paradise* (New York, 1920).

28. Sigourney Fay to FSF, 10 December 1917, Fitzgerald Papers.

29. Turnbull, p. 339.

Chapter 3

1. *Letters*, p. 402.

2. Shane Leslie to FSF, 20 August 1920, Fitzgerald Papers.

3. Citations from "The Diamond as Big as the Ritz" are to *The Stories of F. Scott Fitzgerald*, ed. Malcolm Cowley (New York, 1951). Hereafter cited as *Stories.*

4. James Drawbell, *An Autobiography* (New York, 1964), pp. 173-74.

5. Malcolm Cowley, ed., "Introduction," p. xxii. *Stories.*

6. Citations from the text are to *The Beautiful and Damned* (New York, 1922).

7. Archbishop Austin Dowling to Monsignor O'Hern, 3 June 1921, Fitzgerald Papers.

8. Irene C. Barron to JMA, 27 March 1972.

9. Irene C. Barron to JMA, 11 December 1971.

10. "Funeral Services Are Held Here for Dr. Joseph Barron," *Catholic Bulletin* [St. Paul], 22 April 1939, p. 1.

11. James Michael Reardon, *The Catholic Church in the Diocese of St. Paul* (St. Paul, 1952), p. 243.

12. Monsignor Lawrence O. Wolf to JMA, 9 September 1971.

13. Irene C. Barron to JMA, 23 August 1971.

14. Donald Ogden Stewart, "Recollections of Fitzgerald and Hem-

ingway," *Fitzgerald/Hemingway Annual 1971*, eds. M. J. Bruccoli and C. E. Frazer Clark, Jr. (Washington, D.C., 1971), p. 177.

15. Turnbull, p. 98.

16. Mizener, p. 151.

17. Sister Margaret Mary Burke to JMA, 7 September 1971.

18. Boardman, p. 28. Fitzgerald had in effect left the Church, and in later years he paid little attention to the religious education of his daughter. When they were living in Paris, Fitzgerald did have her study the catechism for a time, but she feels that he did this to please his mother and that his heart was not in it. Mrs. C. Grove Smith to JMA, 26 November 1971.

19. See *Letters,* pp. 182, 184, 529.

20. See Jackson R. Bryer, *The Critical Reputation of F. Scott Fitzgerald* (N.P., 1967), pp. 72, 74-75, 76.

21. Frances Newman, "One of the Wistful Young Men," *F. Scott Fitzgerald in His Own Time: A Miscellany*, p. 371.

See also: John Kuehl, "a la Joyce: the Sisters Fitzgerald's 'Absolution,'" *James Joyce Quarterly*, 2 (Fall 1964), 2-6. Kuehl asserts that "Absolution" derives from Joyce's "The Sisters." As internal evidence he cites in both stories the central relationships of a young boy and a priest, the themes of the betrayal of a child by an adult, and the homosexual tendencies of the priests and their ultimate madness and dissolution.

The circumstantial parallels between the orientations of Joyce and Fitzgerald probably account for the similarities of "Absolution" and "The Sisters" rather than any conscious borrowing on Fitzgerald's part. However, Kuehl's argument for Joyce's direct influence upon Fitzgerald is provocative and is certainly worth considering.

22. Cowley, "Foreword," *Stories*, p. 4.

23. Piper, p. 106.

24. Citations from "Absolution" are to *Stories*.

25. *Sergio Perosa, The Art of F. Scott Fitzgerald* (Ann Arbor, 1969), p. 60.

26. The following fragment from the "Notebooks" (171) places the female destroyer, her mask, her paternity, and the idea of assuming Godhead in a circus setting, and it shows that there was unity in Fitzgerald's thinking about these elements. "She wanted to be ringmaster. ... In somebody else's circus—a father's circus, 'Look here, my father owns this circus. Give me your mask, clown—acrobat, your trapeze....'"

27. It is interesting to note that Fitzgerald considered using the titles "Trimalchio" and "Trimalchio in West Egg" instead of *The Great Gatsby*.

28. Citations from the text are to *The Great Gatsby* (New York, 1925).

29. William Goldhurst, *F. Scott Fitzgerald and His Contemporaries* (Cleveland, 1963), p. 39.

30. See Alexander R. Tamke, "Michaelis in *The Great Gatsby:* Michael in the Valley of Ashes," *Fitzgerald Newsletter*, pp. 304-05.

31. Piper, p. 111.

32. See Bernard Tanner, "The Gospel of Gatsby," *The English Journal*, 54 (September, 1965) 467-74.

Douglas Taylor, *"The Great Gatsby:* Style and Myth," *University of Kansas City Review*, 20 (Autumn 1953), 30-40.

33. Mizener, p. 210.

34. See William Bysshe Stein, "Gatsby's Morgan le Fay," *Fitzgerald Newsletter*, p. 67.

Chapter 4

1. Turnbull, pp. 167-68.
2. Mayfield, p. 116.
3. *Letters*, p. 118.
4. Morley Callaghan, *That Summer in Paris* (New York, 1963), p. 207.
5. George Gent, "Hemingway's Letters Tell of Fitzgerald," *New York Times*, 25 October 1972, p. 38.
6. *Letters*, p. 444.
7. Ibid., p. 368-69.
8. Ibid., p. 337.
9. Citations from "Babylon Revisited" are to *Stories*.
10. Mayfield, p. 161.
11. Fitzgerald, "Handle With Care," *The Crack-Up*, p. 80.
12. Turnbull, p. 234.
13. Citations from "Sleeping and Waking" are to the *The Crack-up*.
14. Charles Marquis Warren to JMA, 25 April 1972.
15. Sheilah Graham, *The Real F. Scott Fitzgerald Thirty-Five Years Later* (New York, 1976), p. 40.
16. *Letters*, p. 102.
17. Ibid., p. 524.
18. Ibid., p. 388.
19. Citations from the text are to *Tender Is the Night* (New York, 1934).

Chapter 5

1. Tony Buttitta, *After the Good Gay Times: Asheville—Summer of '35* (New York, 1974), p. 16.
2. Ibid., p. 45.
3. Ibid.
4. Citations from the articles are to *The Crack-Up*.
5. *Letters*, p. 560.

6. Ibid., p. 577.

7. Ibid., p. 12.

8. Ibid., p. 3.

9. Ibid., p. 23.

10. Ibid., p. 27.

11. Ibid., p. 366.

12. Ibid., p. 365.

13. Ibid., p. 599.

14. Citations from the text are to *The Last Tycoon* (New York, 1941).

15. Fitzgerald, *Tender Is the Night,* p. 204.

16. Mizener, p. 336.

17. Sheilah Graham to Frances Scott Fitzgerald, 14 January 1941, Fitzgerald Papers.

18. Mizener, p. 336.

19. Turnbull, p. 321.

20. In this and the following notes I quote the passage to show the writer's indebtedness to Mizener. Eble, p. 58. "At his death his books were proscribed by the Church, and he was not permitted burial in hallowed ground."

21. Milford, p. 350. "Scott was denied the Catholic burial he had wanted because he had not died within the Church. His books were proscribed."

22. Mayfield, p. 279. "Because he had renounced Catholicism, died without supreme [extreme] unction, and his books had been proscribed, the bishop refused to allow him to be buried in hallowed ground."

23. "Inconspicuous Tombstone Marks Fitzgeralds' Grave," *Asbury Park* [New Jersey] *Sunday Press,* 2 April 1972, 3, p. C8. "... when Fitzgerald died ... the Catholic Church officials stated that Fitzgerald had not died a good Catholic because his books were proscribed by the Church. ..."

24. Arthur Mizener to JMA, 7 December 1971.

25. John Biggs, Jr., to JMA, 10 March 1972.

26. The Reverend Michael J. Arrowsmith, Archdiocese of Washington, D.C., to JMA, 13 February 1972.

27. "Inconspicuous Tombstone. ..," p. C8.

28. Turnbull, p. 322.

29. *Letters,* p. 552.

30. " 'Happy Thought' for the Fitzgeralds," *New York Times,* 8 November 1975, p. 29.

31. Statement on the Occasion of the Burial of F. Scott Fitzgerald, St. Mary's Cemetery, Rockville, Maryland, 7 November 1975. The Reverend Maurice Thomas Fox to JMA, 14 January 1977.

The Fitzgerald Papers

The F. Scott Fitzgerald Papers, which were presented to Princeton University by Fitzgerald's daughter, Mrs. C. Grove Smith, were an important source of material for this book. The collection consists of Fitzgerald's Ledger, scrapbooks, Notebooks, and forty-six large file boxes which contain an extraordinary body of material in various states of organization. The correspondence, which includes letters to and from both the renowned and the obscure, covers the whole range of Fitzgerald's life. Other boxes contain notes and outlines for stories; holograph and typescript manuscripts of stories, novels, poems, and film and radio scripts; reviews and plays; galley proofs and tear sheets; and photographs and miscellaneous papers. The latter have not been catalogued, and they include medical reports, documents concerning insurance and other business matters, some holographs which have not yet been identified by the Princeton staff, passports, school grade reports, and diplomas.

In 1949 Mrs. Smith, who has retained for herself some papers and books, also presented to Princeton Fitzgerald's library of approximately six hundred volumes. Those books which contain inscriptions and/or marginalia were retained in the rare book section, and the others were placed in the stacks.

Index

"Absolution" (Fitzgerald) xii, 9, 12, 14, 44-45, 93-101, 111

Adams, Henry 37

All the Sad Young Men (Fitzgerald) 93, 94

Augustine of Hippo, St. 4-7, 10, 23, 44-45, 48, 72, 73, 74, 89, 97, 101, 102, 109, 138

"Author's House, An" (Fitzgerald) 30, 65

"Author's Mother, An" (Fitzgerald) 2

Autumn in the Valley (Margaret Chanler) 36-37

"Babes in the Woods" (Fitzgerald) 75

"Babylon Revisited" (Fitzgerald) 119-121

Barron, The Rev. Joseph 45, 60, 90-93

Basil (character) 23-25, 29-30, 31-32, 41, 64, 68, 73, 74, 75, 77, 86, 94

Basil Stories (Fitzgerald) 9, 10-12, 18, 21, 23-25, 29-30, 31-32, 41, 63, 68, 74, 119, 129

Baum, William Cardinal 144-145

Beautiful and Damned, The (Fitzgerald) 58, 85, 88-89, 140

Beloved Infidel (Sheilah Graham) 142

Benedict XV, Pope 49-50

"Benediction" (Fitzgerald) 39, 40, 43-45, 91, 95, 102

Benson, Robert Hugh 38, 47, 48, 56, 60, 63, 72

Biggs, Judge John 143

Bishop, John Peale 49, 51, 52, 132

Blaine, Amory *(This Side of Paradise)* 14, 63-64, 66-67, 69, 70-82, 94, 95, 104, 126

Blaine, Beatrice O'Hara *(This Side of Paradise)* 66-67, 69, 71-72, 80, 139

Boyd, Ernest 52

Buffalo, N.Y. 3, 4, 8, 9, 25, 97, 125

Buttitta, Anthony 132-133

Byron, George Gordon 15, 68

Callaghan, Morley 118-119

Carnival imagery xi, xiii, 23-24, 45, 76-78, 81-82, 86-88, 95, 100-101, 102-103, 108, 111-115, 124, 128-131, 134, 135, 139-141, 154n

Carraway, Nick   14, 21, 86, 95, 96, 103, 105-108, 109, 112, 113, 116, 129, 139
Carroll, John (Bishop of Baltimore)   19
Celt and the World, The   (Shane Leslie)   56
Chandelle Jacques ("Shadow Laurels")   16, 69
Chanler, Margaret   36-37, 46, 69-70
City of God   (Augustine)   5-6
City of Man-City of God metaphor   7, 12, 23, 43, 45, 86, 88, 100-101, 102-104, 106, 107, 108, 111-116, 119-120, 124, 125-131, 139-141
Cobb, Humphrey   29
Confessions   (Augustine)   5
Conrad, Joseph   105
Cowley, Joseph   105
Cowley, Malcolm   88, 94
"Crack-Up, The" (Fitzgerald)   133-134
Cullinan, Elizabeth   xiii
Curley, Archbishop Michael   143

Damnation of Theron Ware, The   (Harold Frederic)   72
Darcy, Monsignor   *(This Side of Paradise)*   59, 69-72, 73, 78
"Death of My Father" (Fitzgerald)   63
Delihant, The Rev. Thomas   38-40
"Diamond as Big as the Ritz, The" (Fitzgerald)   85-88
Diver, Dick   9, 14, 63-64, 68, 69, 124-131

"Early Success" (Fitzgerald)   85
Eble, Kenneth   143, 152n, 156n
Esquire   65, 121, 133

Fallon, The Rev. Michael   7-8
Family romance   64-66, 67, 97
Far Side of Paradise, The   (Arthur Mizener)   142
Fay, Alfred Forbes   34-35
Fay, Monsignor Cyril Sigourney Webster   4, 5, 21, 22, 27, 32-33, 34, 35-38, 39, 40, 44, 45, 46-47, 48, 49-50, 55, 56-57, 58-59, 60, 69-71, 72, 92
Fay, Susan Hutchinson   33, 34-35
Fie! Fie! Fi-Fi   (Fitzgerald)   42
Fitzgerald, Annabel   4, 11, 92, 147n
Fitzgerald, Edward   3, 4, 13-14, 15-16, 37, 39, 40, 41, 60, 62, 66, 67, 68, 69, 98-99, 134, 141, 144
Fitzgerald, Frances S. ("Scottie")   60, 92, 118, 119-121, 123, 136-137, 138, 142, 144, 154n
Fitzgerald, Mollie McQuillan   2, 3, 12-13, 14, 15-16, 21, 25, 30, 55, 60-61, 62, 66, 67, 92, 119, 134
Fitzgerald Papers   63, 157
Fitzgerald, Zelda Sayre   45, 50, 57-60, 61-62, 79, 85, 90, 92, 93, 101, 117-118, 119, 121, 132, 134, 138, 144
Flappers and Philosophers (Fitzgerald)   45
Ford, Henry   29, 112
"Forging Ahead" (Fitzgerald)   41
Franklin, Benjamin   33, 104
Frederic, Harold   72

"Freshest Boy, The"
(Fitzgerald) 29-30
Freud, Sigmund 64, 119

Gatsby, Jay xii, 14, 58, 68, 93,
94, 95, 97, 99, 101-116, 126, 129,
140, 142
Great Gatsby, The (Fitzgerald) xi,
44, 93, 95, 99, 101-116, 117, 126,
133, 138, 141, 144
Gibbons, James Cardinal 27-28,
35-36, 39, 49, 58
Grace, Thomas (Bishop of St.
Paul) 20
Graham, Sheilah 72, 123, 137-
138, 142
Greene, Graham xiii, 124

Hackensack, N.J. 27-28
"Handle With Care"
(Fitzgerald) 133, 134-135
Hecker, Isaac Thomas 26-27
Hemingway, Ernest 51, 119, 132,
135
Hemmick, Monsignor
William 46-48, 59, 150n
Hill, James J. 2, 20, 38, 82, 98,
99, 104, 109
Hutchinson, James H. 33-34

"Ice Palace, The" (Fitzgerald) 21
Index Librorum Prohibitorum 143
Ireland. Archbishop John 20, 61,
82

Jefferson, Thomas 33
Joyce, James 21-22, 29, 94, 154n

Keats, John 80, 135
Keneally, Thomas xiii

Key, Grancis Scott 3, 40, 63
King, Genevra 50, 52, 71, 75, 79
Kuehl, John 19, 154n

"La Belle Dame Sans Merci"
(John Keats) 80
Last Tycoon, The (Fitzgerald)
137-141
Ledger (Fitzgerald) 7, 8, 9, 13,
17, 18-19, 23, 30, 31, 32, 50, 59,
60, 64, 97, 98
Leslie, Shane 21, 22, 46-48, 56,
59, 60-61, 62, 70-71, 84, 91,
150n, 151n
Light and candle imagery,
Fitzgerald's use of xiii, 7, 24,
43, 44-45, 78, 79, 95-96, 100-101,
102-103, 114, 120
Locke, Jesse A. 26-27, 38
"Luckless Santa Claus, The"
(Fitzgerald) 31

McHale, Tom xiii
MacKenzie, Compton 48, 63, 72
McQuillan, Annabel 16-17, 26,
41
McQuillan, Philip Francis 2, 15

Marlow (Conrad character) 105
Mask, Fitzgerald's use of xi, 10-
11, 24, 32, 42-43, 54, 73, 75, 77,
79, 80, 106, 110, 112, 129, 131,
147n
Mayfield, Sara 143, 156n
Mencken, H.L. 63, 93, 110
Milford, Nancy 143, 156n
Miller, Rudolph
("Absolution") 12, 24, 96-101,
104, 105, 108, 111, 125, 128

Mizener, Arthur 110, 142-143
Moore, Brian xiii

Nardin Academy 8-9, 97
Nassau Literary Magazine 42, 54, 56, 60
Newman, John Cardinal 27, 48
Newman School 4, 9, 15, 17, 18, 21, 26-31, 32, 38, 41, 46, 48, 58, 64, 86, 122, 148n
"Night at the Fair, A" (Fitzgerald) 23-25, 74, 129
"Notebooks" (Fitzgerald) 17, 20, 154n

Ober, Harold 119, 132, 137
O'Hara, John 22, 136
O'Keefe, Chevalier *(The Beautiful and Damned)* 88-89, 95, 108, 125
"Ordeal, The" (Fitzgerald) 39, 42-43, 44, 95, 96, 102

"Pain and the Scientist" (Fitzgerald) 31
Palms, Stephen ("The Romantic Egoist") 63-65, 69, 97
"Pasting It Together" (Fitzgerald) 135
Patch, Anthony 14, 58, 68, 88, 140
Percy, Walker xiii
"Perfect Life, The" (Fitzgerald) 31-32
Perkins, Maxwell 102, 118, 132
Petronius 101
Piper, Henry Dan 94-95, 104
Poe, Edgar Allan 15, 38, 78
"Pope at Confession, The" (Fitzgerald) 45-46

Portrait of an Artist as a Young Man, A (James Joyce) 94
Princeton University 15, 21, 22, 30, 38, 41-42, 45, 46, 48, 50, 51-52, 55, 57, 60, 62, 63, 71, 72, 74, 75, 90, 143

"Romantic Egoist, The" (Fitzgerald) 55-56, 59, 60, 63-64, 69, 76, 97
Roosevelt, Theodore 36, 38, 40

St. Paul (city) 2, 3, 4, 9, 14, 15, 17, 18, 19-21, 22, 23, 25, 30, 31, 41, 50, 60, 64, 66, 70, 82, 90-91, 92, 93
St. Paul Academy 17, 25-26, 29, 31, 90
St. Paul Cathedral 4, 18, 20, 91
St. Paul Seminary 20, 90-91
Saturday Evening Post 10, 61
Schwarz, Father ("Absolution") 24, 95-96, 97, 100-101, 102, 104, 108, 111, 112, 114, 125, 128, 129, 140
Scribner's 56, 60, 62, 63, 117
"Sentiment and the Use of Rouge" (Fitzgerald) 54-55
"Shadow Laurels" (Fitzgerald) 16, 64, 69
Sheed, Wilfred xiii
Sinister Street (Compton MacKenzie) 48
"Sleeping and Walking" (Fitzgerald) 121-123, 136
Smart Set 60, 93, 94
Spoiled priest 88, 112, 124-128, 131
Stahr, Monroe *(The Last Tycoon)* 15, 138-141
Stern, Milton 152n

Swinburne, Algernon Charles 38, 69, 72

Syneforth, Clay ("Sentiment and the Use of Rouge") 54-55

Taylor, Cecelia 38, 78

Tender Is the Night (Fitzgerald) xi, 9, 69, 117, 121, 123, 124-131, 132, 138

"That Kind of Party" (Fitzgerald) 10-12, 18

This Side of Paradise (Fitzgerald) xi, 22, 36, 48, 56, 59, 60, 61, 62-83, 84, 90, 102, 104, 124, 126

Thompson, Francis 71

Thoreau, Henry David 26

"Thoughtbook" (Fitzgerald) 17-18, 19

Tipton, Terence ("That Kind of Party") 10-12

"Trail of the Duke, The" (Fitzgerald) 31

Trimalchio 101, 108, 113, 114, 135, 154n

Turnbull, Andrew 123, 142, 143, 144

Ulysses (James Joyce) 21, 22

Vatican xiii, 49

Visitation Convent and Academy (St. Paul) 2, 17, 20

Warren, Charles Marquis 123

Washington, George 33, 87

Wilde, Oscar 16, 38, 72, 81

Wills, Garry xiii

Wilson, Edmund 21, 51, 52, 61, 72, 119, 135

Wilson, Woodrow 49

"Winter Dreams" (Fitzgerald) 94

Youth's Encounter (Compton MacKenzie) 48